KEEP ON KICKING AS LONG AS YOU'RE TICKING

Nell W. Mohney
Keep
On Kicking
As Long
As You're
Ticking

Dimensions
FOR LIVING
NASHVILLE

KEEP ON KICKING AS LONG AS YOU'RE TICKING

This book is printed on recycled, acid-free, elemental-chlorine-free paper.

Library of Congress Cataloging in Publication Data

Mohney, Nell.
    Keep on kicking as long as you're ticking / Nell Mohney.
      p. cm.
    ISBN 0-687-08171-8
    1. Christian life—Anecdotes.   2. Mohney, Nell. I. Title.
    BV4517.M64   1999
    242—dc21   98-43829
                                                    CIP

99 00 01 02 03 04 05 06 07 08—10 9 8 7 6 5 4 3 2 1

MANUFACTURED IN THE UNITED STATES OF AMERICA

To my cherished daughter-in-law
Jackie Mohney,
who radiates pure joy in living.
Her presence in our family is like a
lovely benediction.
She is my friend, my confidant, and my encourager
to "keep on kicking as long as I am ticking."

Contents

Foreword

HAVING LUNCH WITH NELL MOHNEY IS AN EXPERIENCE! SHE IS JUST AS pretty and vivacious as she was when she first came to Chattanooga years ago as the wife of the new Methodist minister in town, Dr. Ralph Mohney. "I can't wait to tell you about my interview with Billy Graham," she might say. Or it might be an enthusiastic story about a woman she talked with on a plane last week, or a speaker at a singles conference. Over lunch we would catch up—Nell is ever sensitive—as we discussed the mysteries of life, and God's love and care for us.

The new friend that I met when we were both much younger has become one of my most extraordinary friends, a woman who has made a difference in the lives of thousands of people. I marvel at Nell's energy, and at the influence that she has with audiences all over the country. I love her. I admire her.

The story she tells about my telephone call to her back in 1977 is true. Although she was not a writer, her reputation as a Sunday school teacher who kept her large audience of men and women spellbound had impressed me. I had also heard her speak. We were searching for someone to write a Sunday column for the *Chattanooga Free Press* that would be an inspiring *Guideposts*-type column. I considered several people, but Nell's name kept coming to mind. When I called her, I had no idea that she had been praying for an opportunity in the media for just that thing. That was the year Nell became a writer.

Over the twenty years, we have become dear friends, and each Sunday she tells our readers about an inspiring person who is either battling cancer, depression, or a failed marriage, and who has found the Christian faith to be the answer. Sometimes she interviews an outstanding Christian leader such as Robert Schuller or his wife, Arvella, or a famous gospel singer or a missionary. Subjects for columns seem to appear easily for Nell, whose love for Christ and for people cross all denominational barriers. There was one advertiser who requested his ad always be placed on the same page with

Nell Mohney's column. Many readers cut out her column each week and save it to reread.

This woman with a happy smile has been blessed with both happy and sad times. Her teenage son was killed in an accident. She survived a bout with cancer. I have laughed with Nell and cried with Nell. I have watched her ministry grow. She speaks to Church Growth Conferences, to young people, to various Christian groups in this country and abroad, to corporations, and to civic groups such as the Chamber of Commerce. She writes books.

Nell Mohney is a woman with a gift. She truly walks with God, and it is easy to see. Many times I have said to her, "Nell, the Lord has put his hand on you. There is no other way to explain your life." I am anxious to read over these chapters—the best of Nell Mohney—and to enjoy again the many sides of her character: her compassion, her energy, her enthusiasm, her positive thinking, her openness for adventure, and her deep faith.

Helen Exum
Executive Vice President,
Chattanooga Free Press

Introduction

THE DATE WAS DECEMBER 31, 1977, AND AS I HAD DONE FOR FIFTEEN years, I sat down to write a list of my great expectations for the new year. It was a list I had made thoughtfully and prayerfully for all those years. The idea had originated from an article I had read in *Guideposts Magazine* in 1962. It was the true story of eight middle-aged Christian couples who had met to celebrate New Year's Eve together. One of the men told of reading how our deep expectations affect what actually happens to us—"As he [or she] thinketh in his heart, so is he [or she]" (Prov. 23:7).

The group agreed to try an experiment. They would each write on a three-by-five card one thing they deeply expected to happen to them during the following year. Each placed his or her cards in an envelope, sealed it, and though they could think about the expectation and pray about it, they were not to open the envelope until they were all together the following New Year's Eve.

When they assembled the next year, everyone was present except one man who had died months earlier. His widow was asked to open his envelope first. The man had written: "If I am alive this time next year (both my father and brother died in their forty-seventh year), I expect to learn to listen more sensitively to my wife and our teenage children."

As they continued to open the envelopes, there was such a "coincidence" between their expectations and their actions that it validated the principle for them.

When I read the article, I asked myself, *Is this accurate? Have I missed something in the Christian faith?* To experiment, I listed ten things I deeply longed for—none of them material. I listed ways in which I wanted to grow personally (spiritually, mentally, emotionally, and in physical appearance), relationally (with children, husband, friends, and faculty members in the college where my husband was serving as president), and in my career as speaker, Sunday school teacher, and hostess to guests at the college. When I finished the list, I gave it two tests: Is there anything on this list that will hurt me or anyone else? Is there anything that is not in keeping with the will of God? When the expectations passed those tests, I tossed them heavenward, but consciously thought of them when I awakened each morning, and prayed about them before I went to sleep each evening.

Because I am by nature a "doubting Thomas," I added a "P.S.," in which I listed one small material thing I had never told anyone I wanted. It was a purse-size, magnifying mirror. It was too small to put on a birthday or Christmas list, and I never found one while shopping.

Three months after I had written my list, I accompanied my husband to an education meeting in Boston. One morning, as he returned from a seminar, he said, "I brought you a surprise." When he handed it to me, it was a small, purse-size magnifying mirror. I was stunned! Quickly, I asked, "Have I ever said I wanted this?" With a puzzled look on his face, he said, "No. Don't you like it?"

"Oh yes, I like it, but have I ever suggested that I wanted it?"

Still with a puzzled look on his face, he replied, "No." Curious to know what had prompted him to buy it, I continued to push by asking: "Have I ever even hinted that I wanted it?"

"No," he said impatiently. By this time he must have been wondering why he had bought it, and wishing he hadn't. Then I told him about my list. That incident made me look carefully at the other expectations, and caused me to ask if I really did want them. Through the years, I have prayerfully continued my New Year's Eve ritual. The expectations have enabled me to dream some God-sized dreams.

Then, on New Year's Eve 1977, I listed, among other things: "It is my deep desire to have a television program in which I interview people about their faith—on the *Guideposts* format." Our church congregation had moved into a new sanctuary and educational building, the latter containing a television studio. We telecast our worship service each Sunday, but we wouldn't originate programs for a number of years in the future. So I tossed that dream heavenward, with no thought of an immediate fulfillment. Exactly one week to the day I had written my list, Helen Exum, executive vice president of the *Chattanooga Free Press,* called me with these words:

"Nell, we are thinking of having a regular Sunday feature, and we would like to invite you to write it. Our thought is that you would interview people about their faith—on the *Guideposts* format." The very words I had written. I was stunned into silence.

"Nell, are you there?" asked Helen.

"Yes," I replied as I pulled myself back into reality. Then I told her about my Great Expectations list.

"It's an open door, Nell. Walk through it."

I promised to think about it, pray about it, and let her know in five days. When I walked into her office, I was like Moses—full of excuses. "I don't have enough time," I said. "I don't know that many people; I don't know how to write. So, I have to decline your invitation."

"Nell, write like you speak," said Helen as she figuratively pushed away my excuses. I left her office that day thanking her for the new opportunity. Next to my husband, she is the most persuasive person I have ever met!

In retrospect, I realize what a tremendous blessing this has been to me. I have met people of strong faith, from astronauts to evangelists to senators to actresses to a friend down the street. In addition, I have been forced to think through my own beliefs and articulate my growing faith. Many, many letters from readers have validated my desire for my writings to be a ministry.

My first book, *The Inside Story* (Upper Room, 1979), was a compilation of some of my earliest columns. Now six books and twenty years later, I am responding once again to numerous requests for a collection of some of my favorite columns. It is my prayer that they will bless your life. I hope that they can be used for devotionals, as illustrations in inspirational talks or sermons, and, most especially, that they will meet your heartfelt needs. May God bless you as you read, and on your life's journey.

KEEP ON KICKING AS LONG AS YOU'RE TICKING

1

Keep On Kicking As Long As You're Ticking

A FRENCH WRITER ONCE SAID THAT THERE ARE PEOPLE WHOSE CLOCKS stop at a certain point in their lives. When I reread that statement recently, I began to think of people for whom this is true. For example, Mrs. Gainsay lived three doors down from my family as I grew up. Her house was dark, her clothes were dark, her face was dark. Her clock had stopped twenty years earlier with the death of her only child.

Then there was Harold, who lived with his family on the other side of the street. You never had to wonder what Harold would talk about. No matter what was happening in current, national, or local news, Harold would somehow work into the conversation the college football game in which he made two touchdowns. My dad often commented that if Harold exerted as much energy in his work as in his football fantasies, his family would be much better off. His clock stopped on that football field years earlier.

One of my most earnest prayers is, "Lord, keep me kicking as long as I am ticking." I truly want to wear out, not rust out. Yet it is not always easy to stay energized. Stress, problems, guilt, illness, chronic pain, boredom—all these have a way of stopping our clocks before the body dies. How can we energize ourselves to keep on ticking?

In addition to the energy triangle—adequate rest, good nutrition, and regular exercise—I have found the following suggestions helpful when I need my batteries recharged.

First, I have learned that each morning I have the choice between being energetic or listless, enthusiastic or bored, happy or miserable. In Barbara Johnson's book *Splashes of Joy in the Cesspools of Life* (Word Publishing, 1992), she writes, "Pain is inevitable, but misery is optional." All of us will have problems, disappointments, pain, even tragedy, but we can choose our reactions. Psychologists tell us that the entire day is conditioned by two four-minute periods—the first four minutes when we awaken and the four minutes before we go to sleep.

I am far more energetic during the day if I do two things upon awakening: I first remind myself that each day is a gift from God as I repeat the twenty-fourth verse of Psalm 118: "This is the day which the Lord hath made; [I] will rejoice and be glad in it." Then, I focus on my blessings and give thanks. Finally, I repeat Colossians 1:27 (JBP), and insert my name. "The secret is simply this, Nell Mohney: Christ [is alive] *in you* ... bringing with him the hope of glorious things to come." It is a reminder that I am not alone.

The second way I recharge is to work with my circadian rhythm, or internal clock. For me, the best time for creative work—writing, thinking, speech preparation, and so forth—is from 9:00 A.M. to 2:00 P.M. After that I can handle mundane tasks like cleaning, telephoning, food preparation, and planning.

Third, it helps me feel more energetic if my day is organized before I am catapulted into it. When I organize my week on Sunday afternoon, I follow up each evening with a quick review of my goals and plans for the following day. When I don't do that, my energy is depleted the next morning as I play "catch-up" or try to get organized.

Fourth, I need to commit myself to some project, cause, goal or problem solving task. The energy to do a job seldom comes until you leap into the assignment. Hesitancy never generates energy. Commitment—even reluctant commitment—is often the first step to eliminating fatigue. In pinpointing the time when he made a commitment to comedy as a career, Bill Cosby said, "When you make a commitment, your blood has that particular thing in it, and it's hard for people to stop you."

Fifth, I try to stay positive and keep in touch with positive people. I have several friends from whom I can draw energy just by talking with them on the telephone. Negative people can drain your energy. Also, you can become fatigued by listening to your own mental complaining and worrying.

Finally, I set aside regular times to regenerate the energy supply. I do this through reading, exercise, laughter, time spent with people I love, and most of all through a quiet time for reading God's Word, thinking, and praying. After all, Christ can cure us of negative emotions by filling us with their positive opposites. These joy-generating emotions create vitality and keep us kicking as long as we are ticking.

2

Go for Your Dreams

"CARRAGEN HOUSE IS A CHARMING VICTORIAN BED AND BREAKFAST" and "the best place in town to stay."

Those were the words of a PTA president in Starkville, Mississippi, where I was to speak to parents and students. When I arrived, I discovered that her description of Carragen House was an understatement.

Situated on twenty-two acres of beautiful land near Mississippi State University, the house is approached by a long tree-lined driveway. Even on an afternoon when the skies were overcast and there was a slight drizzle, I had visions of the Old South—plantations where pretty girls strolled the grounds carrying parasols and wearing crinoline-lined dresses.

The house is large and white and has porches that encircle both the upper- and lower-level floors. Inside, the ceilings are high and the furnishings are elegantly authentic. The contemporary touches come in enlarged or newly constructed bathrooms. As impressed as I was by the physical structure, I was more impressed by the owner, Kay Shurden, who is living her dream.

An attractive woman in her midfifties, Kay greeted me warmly at the front door when I arrived. On the bedside table in my room, she had placed a basket of fruit and a platter of freshly baked gourmet chocolate-chip cookies. The room was cozy and inviting and made me feel that I had gone to visit my grandmother. *It is no surprise that this place is so popular*, I thought as I relaxed in the chaise longue before dressing for a dinner meeting. *I wonder how Kay acquired it?*

"It was a God-given dream," she said in answer to that question the following morning. She had joined me on the sunporch for a superb breakfast (orange juice; fresh fruit with a delicate sauce; eggs; Southern-style grits; bran muffins; and coffee). She told me that eight years earlier her husband had died very suddenly of a heart attack. Their two daughters were in college at the time. As Kay walked through the early stages of her grief, she realized that she needed to go to work, not only for monetary reasons, but also to keep her sanity.

Having been reared in a typical Southern household, she had never worked outside the home. Her talents and interests had been in the areas of homemaking—cooking, interior design, and parenting—but no such jobs were readily available. She took a nine-to-five job at a local bank. The people she worked with were kind, and the job wasn't too difficult, but she felt almost imprisoned. In fact, there were times when she felt positively claustrophobic.

A person of deep Christian faith, Kay focused her prayer time on asking God for guidance. "Lord, you know that I need and want to work, but I'm so unfulfilled in this job. What do you want me to do?" Over and over again she found the phrase "Go for your dream" lingering in her mind as she finished her prayers.

One Saturday afternoon, in looking through some personal journals, she found these words she had written some twenty years earlier, after she and her husband had returned from a "bed and breakfast tour" of England: "It is my dream to have a 'bed and breakfast' place someday after the girls are educated. It will allow me to utilize all my talents—cooking creatively, decorating, and being hospitable to people who want a home away from home." In the busy everyday activities of running her home and rearing children, Kay had forgotten she had ever written those words. Yet in her prayer time they were being brought to her remembrance.

When she shared her dream with a longtime friend, her friend said excitedly, "The perfect place is for sale. It is the Carragen House, though it would require lots of renovation."

The story of how the house came into Kay's possession seems miraculous. "God arranged for me to have this house, but God is expecting lots of hard work from me," she explained. Today the business is so successful that a son-in-law has joined her in partnership.

As I arose from the breakfast table that Valentine's Day, she said, "Remember that God gives us all dreams. When the time is right, he pushes us out of the nest with the words 'Go for your dreams.'"

Quietly and reflectively I looked back across the years of my life and I, too, saw God's hand at work making my dreams become a reality. Isn't it true with you?

3

Any Wrinkles on Your Soul?

SOCIAL GATHERINGS DURING THE CHRISTMAS SEASON SEEM ALMOST magical. An ambiance of excitement and anticipation is created by beautifully decorated homes, the sound of carols playing, carefully prepared food, and lively conversation. It was at such a gathering last year that I heard a new and unusually descriptive phrase.

Four of us were chatting while eating hors d'oeuvres and waiting for dinner to be served. Suddenly Robert, a man in his early fifties, walked into the room. Obviously well liked by the people present, he was being described by such adjectives as "friendly," "an astute business leader," "a good family man." Then, one of the women laughingly remarked, "But isn't it disgusting that he hasn't a single wrinkle on his face, while the rest of us discover a new one daily!" We laughed about her comment. Then Robert's business associate remarked thoughtfully, "More important, he has no wrinkles on his soul."

We were interrupted in our conversation when another person joined the group, but the phrase "no wrinkles on his soul" kept tugging on my mind like a dog toying with a neighbor's paper. Later I had the opportunity to ask, "What did you mean when you said that Robert has no wrinkles on his soul?" Settling back into his chair, he replied, "Robert is the most centered man I have ever known. He knows who he is, and his priorities are crystal clear. As a result, he doesn't deplete his energy with petty concerns like grudges or hurt feelings. He can make hard and necessary business decisions, but he does it in a humane way—with sensitivity to the feelings of others, and with fairness.

"Robert listens when others offer him constructive criticism. He doesn't react defensively, but weighs the criticism carefully and then, if he feels it is justified, corrects his course. He learns from his mistakes. In other words, he is amazingly mature emotionally. Also, he has no sense of self-importance. He enjoys life tremendously and has a great sense of humor. In fact, he is fun to work with.

"From my observation, his centeredness comes from a deep religious faith. He is not pious or judgmental, but he is unashamedly a man of faith and prayer, and Robert is an active Christian churchman. It is because he has no wrinkles on the core part of his being— his soul—that the rest of his life seems so free of clutter and tension."

As I listened to this description, it occurred to me that what science and religion have been telling us for the past twenty years about the body-mind-spirit connection is affirmed in Robert's life. If we are to be whole persons, we must have concomitant growth in each of these areas. We must remember that we are basically spiritual beings encased in a flesh-and-blood body house. This body house, according to Paul, is the temple of God. "Do you not know that your body is a temple of the Holy Spirit within you, which you have from God, and that you are not your own? For you were bought with a price; therefore glorify God in your body" (1 Cor. 6:19-20 NRSV).

Yes, the body needs to be cared for and involved in a fitness program. We need to learn anew the importance of nutrition, exercise, and relaxation. Give up the junk food and participate in an exercise program that is appropriate to our age. Let us remember that exercise will not only make our bodies look better, but will sharpen our mental faculties as well.

A part of mental well-being is emotional maturity. So many times I have reminded myself of a quotation by Dr. Hazen Werner: "You are young only once, but you can be immature indefinitely." Give yourself an EMQ (emotional maturity quiz). Ask yourself such questions as, Am I being controlled by negative emotions—anger, fear, resentment, jealousy, negativism, and so forth. Am I firm in my own beliefs, but accepting of and compassionate toward others? Can I give up short-term pleasures for long-term results? Are my values consistent with my actions; do I "walk the talk"? If our answers aren't all that we would like them to be, we can choose one area and begin to work on it until we achieve mastery. Then move on to another.

Finally, our most important work is spiritual fitness. We must be firmly anchored by faith in God, guided by his eternal principles. The practice of spiritual disciplines such as silence, meditation, prayer, the study of the Scriptures, worship, and service pays big dividends. We will not be tossed about by every wind that blows. We will have an inner spiritual gyroscope. We will find that the words spoken by Luke about Jesus can also describe our lives: "Jesus increased in wisdom and in stature, and in favor with God and man (others)" (Luke 2:52 RSV). Only then will we have "no wrinkles on our souls."

4

Three Strikes—Out? No!

SOME PEOPLE ENTER A ROOM AND THE ENTIRE ROOM SEEMS TO LIGHT up. Jane is definitely one of those persons. She is vibrantly alive. Recently when she played the piano and led singing at an evangelism conference, everybody felt better. The secret of her vibrancy is found in her authentic faith, which is based on bedrock trust in God and expressed in a naturally "bubbly" personality. Yet her personality hasn't always bubbled, and her faith has been less than staunch. She is convinced that it is often through the crises of life that God shows us "a more excellent way." Doors to a deeper faith opened after three such crises in her life.

The first was the death of her mother when Jane was only seventeen and a freshman in college. Being a midlife child was like being an only child, and she and her mother were best friends. Her mother's death from cancer was devastating to Jane; yet it was then that she began to discover God as the source of real comfort and hope.

When she was thirty, she had a successful life in the palm of her hand. She was happily married, the mother of two healthy children, and the associate producer of the network TV show *Name That Tune*. The songs she had written were sung by such well-known vocalists as Julius LaRosa and Eartha Kitt. Her scripts and music were used in the off-Broadway theater that she and her husband owned and that she managed. It seemed obvious that for her "the sky was the limit."

So, the words of the physician cut through her consciousness like a knife: "You have cancer and must have surgery immediately." It was like a death sentence, because at that time she knew no one who recovered from cancer.

On the night following surgery, her husband had gone home to be with the children, and she was all alone. She was filled with fear and self-pity. Into her anxious and almost panicked mind a scripture verse seemed to float from nowhere. The words were used by a father whose son was seriously ill: "I believe; help thou mine unbelief" (Mark 9:24). As Jane began to say those words, a feeling of great peace came over her. She recalled, "I felt as if someone were holding my hand. Then I heard—no not heard, but felt the following words: 'I love your family more than you do, so if I ask you to be with me, I'll take care of them." She fell into peaceful sleep immediately.

When she recovered and resumed her activities, she did remember God's blessings enough to agree to be the church organist. Still, she was only a Sunday Christian until a Lay Witness Mission came to her church. She only attended that weekend because she had to play the piano. What she heard, however, changed her life. These were ordinary people, not professional speakers, but Christ was as real to them as their next-door neighbors. They had something she wanted, and she asked Christ to "become boss in my life."

She continued, "With my flare for dramatics, I was sure that God would make me a female Billy Graham. He didn't do that, but he did lead me to another woman in our church and we became the 'Jane and Janet Singing Duo' to bear witness to his love and power."

The third crisis came one night when she walked out of the stage door and found her husband waiting for her. She knew that something was wrong, but she was stunned to learn that their seventeen-year-old son had been arrested for possession of marijuana. "We were a close family and talked about everything, including drugs," she said. "How could our son do this? I felt sick, helpless."

The arresting officer told them that it was obvious that their son was just experimenting. Yet, to teach him a lesson, he was kept in a children's shelter for a week. It proved to be a blessing in disguise. What he saw there opened his eyes and set his directions for the future. His grades, which had been mediocre, improved to the point that he received a full college scholarship. He also received a graduate degree and is now a college professor. It was in that crisis that Jane found the ministry that God had in mind for her. The seed was sown in the courtroom where she saw young people being treated like pieces of garbage, with no family member present to support or care for them. Later she heard Chuck Colson tell of his prison ministry. She said to him, "I'm a professional musician, but more important, I am a Christian. If I can help in your program, I want to."

She now leads the singing and is part of the teaching ministry in the Colson three-day Bible seminars in state and federal prisons across the nation. "In many ways," she reported, "the church inside the prison is more alive than the church outside. The corps of Christians inside the walls are helped through the power of Christ to relate to the others in love instead of hate, in forgiveness instead of resentment. Lives are being changed."

She concluded our interview with a joyous declaration: "When I went to New York thirty years ago, I wanted to be rich and famous. I am that now—in God's kingdom. All of the glitter of show business cannot compare with the joy of seeing Jesus change lives."

5

Had Any Planned Surprises?

Many years ago my husband and I learned the value of "planned surprises." When children are young, life can be hectic—lots of spills to clean up, noses to wipe, diapers to change, squabbles to settle, and noise to endure. For the primary caregiver, the tasks seem endless. Recognizing this, my husband devised a wonderful solution. He would plan something for me to look forward to every two weeks. At times it was a dinner out for the two of us; at other times it was a family outing, such as a picnic, or swimming, or skating. We all looked forward to these events, and as the children got older, they helped plan them.

It didn't take us long to understand the value of this idea. First, everyone was happier when we had something to look forward to. You can take anything for two weeks! When we had two cases of chicken pox at once, and I had had little sleep for days, I didn't lose my cool, because I could say to myself, *Only four more days and I'll be getting out.* When the children needed a change of focus, we would play the guessing game about where we would be going for our family outing. In retrospect, I realize that because of these events we had far more fun and quality time as a family. Certainly, I had warm feelings of appreciation for my husband, who in the midst of a busy pastorate, had used time, effort, and imagination for "planned surprises."

The memory of those events and their value came vividly to mind when I experienced two surprises over the same Valentine's weekend. On February 14, I was returning to Chattanooga from a speaking engagement at a Family Life Event in Starkville, Mississippi. Torrential rain in Starkville and in Atlanta had caused delays in flights so that my plane was late arriving in Chattanooga.

Although I was pleased that Ralph had planned for us to have dinner out, I was so tired that I thought take-outs would be great. "We'll be leaving in an hour," he said cheerily as he deposited my bag in the bedroom. "Where are we going?" I asked. "Haven't decided," he replied, grinning slyly. That should have given me the clue that this wasn't as unplanned as he had led me to believe. I was looking in the mirror at my limp hair and my rain-splattered makeup when he called out, "Wear your red dress." *My red dress?* I thought wearily. *I look more like I should be wearing jeans than a red dress.*

En route to dinner, Ralph pretended to stop at the Read House and then the Marriott, but found some excuses for not staying at either. As he pulled out on Broad Street, I laughingly said, "Remember that I'm all dressed up!" Smiling, he drove directly to South Side Restaurant, where lots of people were in line for the first of two seatings for the evening. Walking past them, we went directly to "our" table, where our son and his wife were already seated. Having them join us was another of my husband's planned surprises. We had a great time visiting while we ate; and just before dessert, there was another of his surprises. He had arranged for Dave Abercrombie and his Barber Shop Quartet, all dressed in red jackets, tuxedo shirts, with red bow ties, to appear at our table. They brought me a long-stemmed red rose, a box of chocolates, and a Valentine.

Then they sang two love songs. Everyone around us joined in the applause. It was a wonderful evening! The result? My fatigue was replaced by excitement, appreciation for my husband and family, and new motivation to be better in my many roles.

Then on February 16 I went to the Sunday school class where I serve as one of the teachers. On that day—the Sunday after Valentine's Day—I had invited Ray and Georgianna to present a dialogue on "love." In a cleverly planned surprise, they turned the dialogue into a tribute to me and had participation from other members of the class. The result? Although I was a little embarrassed as I listened to all the nice things that were said (I told them later that I felt as if I had been to my funeral), I was also filled with deep gratitude, and a determination to be a better teacher, a more authentic Christian, and a stronger friend.

So, if you have not put some planned surprises in your life, try it. The results are magical!

6

Ever Been Locked Out?

"My mother locked me out of the house," said a tall young woman who is now herself a mother of three. Karen told me of growing up as an only child in a family where parents fought verbally every day for eighteen years of her life until they were divorced.

"In retrospect," said Karen, "I know that my mother had an emotional illness, but I loved her devotedly and was very dependent upon her, especially since my father was away from home so much of the time. Life was unsettled when she became angry, and as a child I tried to do everything I could to please her—being obedient, making good grades, being cheerful. Some days it would work, but other days the least little thing would set her off. The problem was that I never knew whether this was to be a good day or a bad day. As a result, I always felt as if I were walking on eggshells."

During her high school years, Karen was hospitalized on three occasions for ulcerated colitis. Finally, the doctor said to her parents, "If you two don't stop fighting and putting this girl under stress, you are not going to have a daughter." Her stability came through participation in her church's youth group and choir. Having played the piano since her grandmother taught her to play "Jesus Loves Me" when Karen was five years old, Karen developed her musical ability so rapidly that she chose to major in music performance in college.

In the middle of her college freshman year, her mother telephoned and was sobbing uncontrollably. "What is it, Mother?" Karen asked. When her mother caught her breath, she fairly screamed, "He left me. Your dad has left me." Speaking calmly and carefully, Karen replied, "Mother, you knew it was coming. You two have been fighting for years." But that was the wrong response. Her mother raved on and on. Finally, she demanded that Karen call her every day. Although it was the middle of the concert season, Karen promised. She still honored her mother and sought to help her.

In the summer following her junior year, Karen was working each day and living with her mother. One night the parents of the young man whom Karen was dating invited her to their house for dessert, and to watch a movie. Karen's mother didn't like the idea. When Karen returned two and a half hours later, the lights were out and the doors were locked. She had not disobeyed, and she wasn't late, but she was locked out of her own home! She finally went to her father (who had remarried) and asked to spend the night at their apartment. Permission was granted. She tried to call her mother, but there was no answer. The following morning, Karen needed to get into the house and change clothes for work.

When she telephoned her house, it was as if another person answered. "Good morning," said a cheery voice.

"Mom, I need to come over and change clothes."

"Okay, honey, come on over."

It was as if the events of the night before had not occurred. That night Karen got up the courage to say, "Mom, we can't continue like this. I just can't take this uncertainty."

With fury spewing from her eyes and words, Karen's mother replied, "Pack all your clothes and leave this house by eight o'clock in the morning and never come back!"

So, as a college junior, Karen was on her own. She rented a room and continued to work and go to church. Her mother sold the house and moved out of town. Karen didn't see her again for fifteen years. As bad as that rejection was, it was not as devastating as what happened next. Her father was not a Christian, but he and his new wife came to church each time Karen sang or gave an organ recital. Karen was thrilled! Maybe her dad would find the solace and joy she had found in faith.

After their fourth visit, the pastor saw Karen in the hall and asked, "Are your dad and his wife planning to join this church?"

"I don't know sir. Why do you ask?"

"Well, your mother has telephoned one of our deacons, and if your dad seeks membership, it will be denied."

Karen couldn't believe what she had just heard. Where was the love of Christ? Where was forgiveness and a desire to reach others in Christ's name? It was the ultimate betrayal. All her life Karen had tried to do what was right, and it hadn't worked. She decided to leave the church. She continued to work, but didn't have enough money for her senior year at college. She didn't care anymore. Her life had crumbled beneath her! She looked for acceptance any way she could find it. Six months later she was pregnant. The father of the child was willing to pay for an abortion but would take no other responsibility.

At first Karen agreed to the abortion, though she felt it was wrong. One night she had a dream in which the Lord himself stood before her. He assured her that he had always loved her and that though she had made a mistake, she was forgiven. Then he reminded her that two wrongs do not make a right, and asked her to give this child the love she never had. "But what about that minister?" she asked from somewhere deep inside her. "He does not represent my spirit of love and forgiveness," was the kind reply.

Karen awakened with a sense of peace and of being loved unconditionally. She knew that she would not have an abortion. When she told her father, he became irate and insisted that if she didn't have an abortion he would not help her. It was not easy to stand with her conviction. But she did. It was necessary for her to work every day for the nine months before her beautiful baby daughter was born.

Karen joined another church, determined to rear her child in the faith that once again brought support and direction to her life. Her prayer that her father would love her daughter was answered abundantly. The little girl became the "apple of his eye." The end of the story is that Karen is now married to a truly Christian man who adopted her daughter. He and Karen have two other children. Although her mother has changed little, if at all, they see each other occasionally. Karen has forgiven her. Today, Karen uses her music to bless others and to glorify the one who saved her from a life of despair and bitterness.

7

Don't Stop Before the Finish Line

IT WAS A BITTER COLD DAY IN APRIL WHEN MY FRIEND SHERRY RAN in the Boston Marathon. A native of North Carolina, Sherry began jogging at age forty-three. Though she had run in several local races, she was far from being an Olympic competitor.

Yet when her twenty-five-year-old neighbor, Laura, mentioned that she had registered for the Boston Marathon, Sherry was hooked. Alternating between excitement for the event and feelings of "I am too old for that kind of race," Sherry finally reasoned that she would never be any younger. If she were ever to "go for the gold" it was now or never.

Neighbors joined the excitement and had a large bon voyage party for the two women on the eve of their departure. It was a dinner party complete with toasts, a starting gun, and a huge picture of a photo finish for the "Goldsboro Girls." The thrill of the adventure stayed with Sherry and Laura throughout their flight to the historic city.

On Monday morning when thousands of Americans were frantically preparing tax forms for their midnight deadline, Sherry and Laura were leaving their hotel for orientation at the registration center in downtown Boston. Shivering in the 30-degree weather and surrounded by hundreds of young, aerobically exercised bodies, Sherry found herself living with an unspoken question: "What in the world am I doing here?" The question grew louder and louder as starting time approached.

Then, they were off and running! In the beginning it wasn't too bad—much like the races in North Carolina, only five times larger.

As the pace picked up, so did Sherry's fatigue. By the time she was at the halfway point, every muscle in her body ached, she was shivering from cold, and her endurance was on a sit-down strike. *This is a good place to drop out,* she thought to herself. *After all, I've run an acceptable race.*

It was at that strategic moment that the oft-repeated advice of her mother began to flash in Sherry's mind like a neon sign: "Don't stop before the finish line."

Her mother had given that advice to her three children, saying it was applicable for every new venture they undertook. When Sherry wanted to give up piano and drop out of Scouts, her mother said firmly, "Don't stop before the finish line." That didn't mean that the children were committed to an endeavor for a lifetime. Her mother had designated one year as the finish line for a new activity. That period of time took them over the times of frustration and boredom that come from learning a new sport or adjusting to a new organization. Today, Sherry is a talented pianist and serves as a Girl Scout leader because of a mother who encouraged her daughter not to stop before the finish line.

On April 15, 1996, Sherry made it to the finish line—and far ahead of several dozen others. She was huffing and puffing and aching, but she made it! Being able to "hang in there" gave that North Carolinian great satisfaction!

When she laughingly told me that story, I thought about how applicable it is for many of life's endeavors. How many of us have given up on new job opportunities, marriages, learning new skills, or working through problems because of frustrations or boredom. We simply don't give it 100 percent effort. We waver, run out of steam, and lack one of life's most important skills—perseverance. Many have succeeded in the race of life because they refused to quit, and just kept on keeping on.

The apostle Paul overcame difficulties that would defeat most of us—shipwreck, beatings, persecutions, imprisonment. Still, at the climax of that marvelous life, he was able to say, "I have fought a good fight, *I have finished my course,* I have kept the faith" (2 Tim. 4:7 italics added). An inspiration to all who read of his life, Paul didn't stop before the finish line, and neither should we.

8

Are You Circling?

"LIFE IS LIKE CIRCLING PHILADELPHIA," SAID CYNTHIA, A SPEAKER AT a retreat for women. Tall, relaxed, persuasive, this wife, mother, grandmother, and Christian author was suggesting that it is easy to circle life without really living it.

She told of the stresses of early marriage and her life as a mother of three children under three. "The high point of my day was finally being able to go to bed at night."

One day she said to herself, "If going to bed is the high point of my day, why do I even bother to get up?" A desperate prayer was wrung from her heart—"O God, I need purpose in my life. What do you want me to do?" The answers she discovered have been published in a Bible study entitled "Living as a Woman of Purpose."

On a recent flight to Philadelphia, where she was to speak, the fog necessitated their circling the city for more than thirty minutes; she remembered her experience as a young mother. Cynthia observed that the reactions of fellow passengers to the delay that day were symbolic of our reactions to life. The man across the aisle became physically ill as they continued to circle. She reflected that many people are sick of life: They get up each day, go through the routines, return home to watch television, and are tired of the meaninglessness of their lives.

The man who sat beside her reacted angrily. He complained loudly about being late for an appointment, as if he were the only person on the plane who had a schedule. He attacked the airline, as if it were responsible for the weather. In general, he made himself and everyone else miserable. In life, there are people who run around in circles, all the while complaining loudly enough for their negativism to destroy their own peace of mind and that of fellow travelers.

A woman in the seat ahead of Cynthia quickly put on her earplugs, closed her eyes and withdrew into her own world. In daily living, there are people who no longer choose to be engaged in life. They are not interested in people or events around them. While pulling away for periods of rest and spiritual refreshment are important for balanced living, a continuous disengagement from life keeps us from using our talents or making a contribution.

The fourth response, said Cynthia, is to use our best thinking and guidance in a situation and then trust God for the outcome. She said that it is God who gives purpose to and orchestrates life.

Portraying God as the lighthouse, she used Frank Koch's famous illustration of the captain of the battleship being informed by the lookout that there was a steady light bearing on the starboard bow of the ship (*Proceedings,* the Naval Institute). That could only mean they were on a collision course. The captain ordered the signalman to send the following message: "We are on a collision course; advise that you change course 20 degrees."

Immediately the reply returned: "Advisable for *you* to change course 20 degrees."

From the battleship went the message, "I am the captain; change your course."

The reply: "I am a seaman second class; you had better change your course."

The captain was furious. He spat out, "I am a battleship. Change your course!"

Back came the flashing light: "I am a lighthouse." The battleship, of course, changed its course.

The speaker indicated that we like to be in control of everything, but need to remember that God is the lighthouse. She listed three qualities of our Sovereign God that give her life purpose and make her want to get up in the morning. The first is God's unconditional love. She said, "When we finally understand it, we no longer have to manipulate others to get them to love us." She quoted C. S. Lewis: "Don't let your happiness depend upon another person."

The second characteristic is that God is good, though his definition is different from ours. Our definition is "anything that makes us happy"; his is "anything that strengthens our character and makes us more like Christ."

The third characteristic is that God asks us to give glory to him.

Most people, she suggested, want to bring glory to themselves. She said that she had just seen a T-shirt that read, "Please don't treat me any differently than you would the queen."

Some people like to bring glory to others. The Japanese cult members who used poison gas in the subway did it to bring glory to Asahara; and many Americans, she believes, continue to bow at the shrine of Elvis Presley.

"It is only when we recognize the love and goodness of God and seek to bring glory to him that we can stop circling, and live purposefully," said Cynthia. Her peaceful and authentic manner makes her credible.

9

Is Your Angel Nearby?

DURING THE WEEK BEFORE CHRISTMAS, KATHY WAS DISTRAUGHT about a court case in which she was involved. One day as she left her attorney's office, she dissolved in tears. Though she was wearing sunglasses when she entered the elevator, tears were streaming down her cheeks.

"There was an angel on that elevator," Kathy told me during a telephone conversation. The angel was Joanna, a beautiful woman in her early twenties, who was on her way down from the Walden Club. A student at the University of Tennessee at Chattanooga, she had the most dazzling smile, which enveloped Kathy in its warmth.

"Sensing my need, she talked quietly and encouragingly to me, saying things like, 'Don't be discouraged. God will take care of you.' By the time she had walked me to my car, my entire perspective had changed. I had moved from despair to hope, from confusion to clarity in my thinking. As I drove home, I said to myself, 'Kathy, I think you have just had a visit from a Christmas angel.'"

As I reflected on our conversation, I realized anew the continuing interest in angels. For many years, there was little written on the subject, but suddenly bookstores are filled with angel books. Gift shops have angel pins, angel cards, angel Christmas decorations. Even television capitalized on the interest. I have enjoyed *Touched by an Angel*, starring Roma Downey as angel Monica, and Della Reese as Tess, the head angel. The two characters are sent to protect, guide, encourage, and comfort human beings who are struggling in real-life situations today. It is a program that emphasizes strong moral values and religious faith.

What is an angel? Webster defines an angel as "a messenger from God; a supernatural being characterized by more than human power or influence; a guiding spirit or influence." The Bible teaches us that God's Holy Spirit has been given to guide and empower us. In addition, the Bible, in nearly three hundred different places, indicates that God has countless angels at his command. While it doesn't give much specific information about them, it does say that they will be a source of comfort and strength in every circumstance. Dr. Billy Graham describes angels as "created spirit beings who can become visible when necessary."

As I look back on my own life, I realize that the many angels (messengers of God) who have blessed my life have all been visible and known to me. Just when I needed a word of encouragement or hope, or when I needed help with a difficult situation, these angels have appeared in the form of friends or family members. When it happens, I always remember a bit of anonymously written verse:

> When God comes to me on quiet, catlike feet,
> Why am I surprised that it is my neighbor down the street?

Among the many documented angel stories I have read—including the British express train carrying Queen Victoria that was stopped short of a washed-out bridge by a "winged figure," and Eddie Rickenbacker's belief that an angel provided food for him and his B-17 crew who survived for weeks on a life raft in the Pacific—none is more graphic than the one carried in *Reader's Digest* years ago.

According to the story, a neurologist was suddenly awakened one night by someone knocking on the door. He opened it to find an upset little girl, who told him her mother was ill. The girl asked the doctor to follow her. It was a snowy night and bitterly cold. Though exceptionally tired, the doctor got dressed and followed the girl.

The doctor found that the mother had pneumonia. He arranged for medical care, then complimented the woman on how smart her little girl was. The woman looked at him strangely and said, "My daughter died a month ago. Her shoes and coat are in the clothes closet there."

Surprised and puzzled, the doctor went to the closet. There he found that same coat worn by the little girl who had led him to her mother. It was warm and dry, and could not possibly have been out in the bitterly cold and snowy night. In the intervening years, the doctor wondered if in that hour of desperate need he had been called by an angel who appeared as the woman's daughter.

At Christmas, when we sing of "herald angels" and "a heavenly host of angels," let us remember that we are not alone on the planet Earth. The message of Christmas is that God, through Christ, is with us. His messengers, in varying forms will be dispatched to guide, protect, and comfort us. "Glory to God in the highest."

10

Are You a Compulsive Person?

ARE YOU A COMPULSIVE PERSON? YOU ARE PROBABLY THINKING, "I AM a perfectly normal person. Why ask me a question like that?"

That's precisely what I thought until I read Sandra Simpson LeSourd's well-documented and fascinating book *The Compulsive Woman* (Chosen Books, 1987). Before reading the book, I had identified compulsive behavior only with alcoholism, gambling, and drug addiction. According to Sandra, the definition of compulsion given by Compulsivity Clinics of America is "an instant, repetitive, intrusive, and unwanted urge to perform an act that is contrary to one's standards." This can include overeating, undereating, smoking, shopping sprees, relationships or sexual dependencies, perfectionism, prescription drugs, workaholism, and addiction to television.

Obviously, most of us are victims of, or candidates for, one of the above. Yet, unless we confront the problem it could turn into an addiction. The question is, What can we do to correct this—to become integrated, balanced human beings?

Before answering the questions, Sandra tells the story of her own compulsivity. Formerly a contestant in the Miss America Pageant, a Walt Disney artist, and coordinator of the Miss America Pepsi-Cola scholarship, Sandra had a whirlwind romance and marriage to a prominent doctor. They had three lovely children. How could someone who was living the American dream find herself trapped in a life of cross-addictions?

For many years she hid her compulsive behavior behind a charming facade of wittiness, good works, and good looks. Yet, as so often happens, when the cause of compulsive behavior goes untreated, the compulsion grows into addiction—not just one, but cross-addictions. For Sandra, these included nicotine; alcohol; prescription drugs; rigid perfectionism; civic and social "busyness"; overeating; shopping binges; and even cults.

It was as if she were walking through a maze. As soon as she broke free of one addiction, another seemed to reach out and draw her into its trap. Perhaps the most destructive one was her journey into the occult. Ironically, she was drawn into it because of its promise of peace of mind. Yet her continued visits to spiritualists, to hypnotists, to fortune-tellers, and her dependency on the daily horoscope created havoc in her sensitive spirit.

She began to hear hostile, angry voices in her mind. No matter how busy she stayed or how much she drank, there was no quieting of the voices. In desperation, she attempted suicide. Locking herself in the bedroom, she took an overdose of prescription drugs. Fortunately, her teenage daughter came home early from school, broke the window, and entered her mother's room. Though Sandra remained unconscious for twenty-four hours, and though doctors were not encouraging about her survival, she not only lived, but had no brain damage. For her, however, this was just another failure.

"I felt sick, despairing," she reports. "I couldn't even succeed in killing myself! I had reached the bottom of the pit."

In a subsequent hospitalization, Sandra met Karen, a young woman whose fiancé had been killed two weeks before their wedding day. Karen had come to the psychiatric hospital for help in working through her trauma. The words Karen used when she cried out in her grief caught Sandra's attention. How often Sandra heard "Help me, Jesus, please help me." Through the weeks that followed, Sandra watched as this strong faith in Christ worked like a magnet to integrate the brokenness of her new friend. When Karen left the hospital well ahead of schedule, Sandra longed for such a faith.

Upon Sandra's return home, she very slowly began to come to faith. She attended worship and Bible study, and in a healing service in her church, she experienced inner cleansing and a healing of painful memories. A part of this wholeness has come through a compulsivity clinic in which she discovered the causes of her compulsive behavior and a step-by-step way out. She also has learned to forgive herself, to like herself, and to recognize the potential that God has placed within her.

The book is an exciting story in which she tells how, after several years of singleness, she met and fell in love with Leonard LeSourd. Though most of us won't have as many extremes of imbalance in our lives, all of us can benefit by reading her book.

11

Are You What You Think About?

ONCE WHILE SPEAKING IN HIGH POINT, NORTH CAROLINA, I MET A woman who was badly crippled by rheumatoid arthritis, yet I have never met anyone with a sharper mind. Her varied interests made her a sparkling conversationalist, and her concern for others was obvious in the sensitive way in which she drew them into the conversation.

Seated beside this amazing woman was a younger woman whose physical beauty was marred by tension in her face, negativism in her thinking, and a self-centered focus on trivia. For example, while the older woman conversed easily about world events and entertained us with humorous stories, the healthy young woman complained about planes being late, a dent in her new car, and poorly made tennis rackets.

Emerson once said, "A person is what he thinks about all day." It was Paul, the great apostle, who after listing a series of beautiful and worthy ideas said, "Think on these things." Perhaps no one in religious history, other than Jesus, gave more evidence than Paul of having won the major victory of disciplining his own thoughts.

Relatively few of us are able to choose the time in which we live, and many of the externals of life are beyond our control. Yet all of us can control our thinking and choose the things which occupy our minds. As we do so, we create the world in which we live. It is very easy to live in the underworld of our minds, feeding on hatred, envy, jealousy, lust, bitterness, or despair. For the person who is determined to think negatively, there is little anyone on the outside can do.

Do you remember the old story of the man who went trudging down a dusty road? A kind traveler offered him a ride and tried to start a conversation.

"It's a beautiful day we're having," the traveler said, trying to get a conversation going.

"Yes," the man muttered, glancing up at the sky, "but it looks like a weather breeder to me."

"Well, I guess we could stand a little rain, couldn't we? It would be good for the crops."

"Not for the berries, it wouldn't be good," the man moaned.

"You have your place in berries?" the traveler asked.

"Nope! I got my place in corn."

"Well, it looks like we're going to have the best corn crop we've had in years, doesn't it?"

"Yes, but a big crop is awful hard on the land."

For one determined to be disappointed, content with catastrophe, preferring bad news to good news, there can be no heaven. Such a person lives in a homemade hell.

To go out every morning with our minds occupied with difficulties is to invite defeat at the beginning of the day. To fill our minds with thoughts of ill will, grievances, reminders of injuries suffered, is to court failure.

The important thing to remember is the simple fact that all of us choose the things we think about. It is impossible to ruin the day for one who is determined to dwell on the high, the fine, the splendid, and the true.

"I do not allow myself to think terrible things about other people," said a wise old Christian as he listened to a cynic speaking critically of some good folk. "If I let myself think things like that, I might get to believing them, and that would ruin me. It would not make any difference in the people I was thinking about, but it would make a terrible difference in me."

From the moment we awaken in the morning to that hour when we slip off into sleep at night, every thought that comes knocking at the door of our minds is admitted as a guest or refused admission as an enemy, and we make the decision. We are the gatekeepers of our minds. If undesirable characters get inside, it is because of our indulgence or indifference. Paul was right when he wrote, "Finally, brethren, whatsoever things are true, whatsoever things are honest, whatsoever things are just, whatsoever things are pure, whatsoever things are lovely, whatsoever things are of good report; if there be any virtue, and if there be any praise, think on these things" (Phil. 4:8).

12

Said "Thank You" Today?

GRATITUDE OPENS YOUR HEART TO LIFE, TO OTHERS, TO GOD. Ingratitude snaps it shut, and causes you to take for granted the blessings of your life, including the kindnesses offered by friends and family. This fact was confirmed for me by an incident that happened years ago but is still fresh in my memory.

It happened during the noon hour when one of Chattanooga's large department stores was crowded with shoppers. I had stopped in the women's department to pick up a blouse when I became fascinated by a real-life drama. A high school senior had chosen a long, white formal for her senior prom. She was walking through the department modeling it as she awaited her mother's arrival and, hopefully, her approval for the purchase of the gown.

Before her arrival, we onlookers for this unfolding drama learned from a salesperson that the mother was a single parent who had the sole support of four children, the oldest of whom was the senior in the beautiful dress. During her very limited lunch hour, the mother rushed into the department store. Though we spectators pretended to be looking at blouses and dresses, we were as mesmerized by the scene as some people are by soap operas. We couldn't leave the store without learning the outcome.

As the fatigued woman dropped into a chair, we heard her exclaim, "Susan, you do look beautiful in that dress." Her daughter's quick response was, "Then may I have it?" Motioning for her daughter to come closer, the mother took a look at the price tag. Sadly, she shook her head, saying, "Oh, Susan, we just can't afford that." Susan began to plead and beg and promise to do everything from washing dishes to taking care of her younger siblings if her mother would buy the dress.

Finally, the tired-looking woman said, "All right. I'm sure that everyone in the family will be glad to eat hot dogs for a month so you can have it." But instead of giving her mother a grateful hug, or even saying "thank you," Susan rushed to the dressing room and returned with some expensive shoes, an elegant bag, and several other things she wanted. Her mother said firmly, "No, Susan. We can't afford those right now."

At this point, the daughter had a full-blown temper tantrum—yelling and screaming accusations at her mother, who left the store in tears. The onlookers turned away in embarrassment and disgust. Even Susan was unhappy.

A simple "thank you" could have transformed a generous act into a gracious experience. Ingratitude made it an ugly and destructive experience.

Each of us has the power to bring encouragement and joy to others through the simple act of gratitude. Recently, my fatigue turned to elation through such an act. Following my husband's surgery for knee replacement, I was happily and joyfully on duty as night nurse for the seven days he was hospitalized, and full time during the long weeks of therapy. Even so, I was bone tired.

Though he had said "thank you" daily, my husband's gratitude was accentuated when he announced a "Be Nice to Nellie Week." He arranged an out-of-town getaway in one of my favorite cities to say "thank you" in a more formal way. En route, he produced a large leather-bound presentation book entitled "Letters of Appreciation Received by Nell Mohney." Through the years, and without my knowledge, he had filed letters I had received from people who had written appreciatively about one of my columns, a seminar I had conducted, or a kindness expressed. I was overwhelmed! Memories crowded my mind and tears flowed down my cheeks as I read the letters. Suddenly I didn't feel tired anymore. Gratitude had transformed fatigue into sheer joy.

13

Save Us from the Gnats

THE TROUBLE WITH LIFE IS THAT IT IS SO DAILY! WHEN I LOOK AT myself and observe others around me, I see that most of us go through the big crises and traumas with flying colors. The experience may be heart-wrenching, but we are able to marshal all our resources and meet big difficulties with poise and power. It is the small, daily incidents, interruptions, and pressures that sabotage us.

Some years ago a man walked across the United States. He began the journey in California and ended it in New York. At the end of the journey, one reporter asked, "What was hardest for you—the desert, the mountains, or the rivers?" Without a moment's hesitation, the hiker replied, "It was neither of those. The thing that bothered me most was sand in my shoes."

We are often like that. It's the little things that tear us apart. What destroys marriages? Little things! What alienates families? Little things! What is the difference between success and failure? Little things! What troubles a church or community or a nation? Often it is an accumulation of little things—"sand in our shoes."

Several years ago I heard Wayne Dyer, well-known lecturer and author, speak on "How to Be a No-Limit Person." He told a funny story of the man who commuted two hours to and from work each day in bumper-to-bumper traffic. When he was very irritable with the children, they would ask, "What's wrong with Daddy?" The mother would reply, "It's the traffic that makes him that way." When the man went to the hospital with a bleeding ulcer, the children asked, "Why is Daddy in the hospital?" "It's the traffic," replied the mother. Several years later when the man actually died of a heart attack, someone asked his elementary aged son what caused his father's death. Very seriously the young son replied, "It was the traffic."

We may smile at the child's assumption, but we know that little worries, nagging anxieties, and frustrating annoyances can destroy us physically as well as emotionally. Surely there is wisdom in the prayer, "Lord, we can handle the elephants, but please deliver us from the gnats."

In one of his earliest books, the late Harry Emerson Fosdick told the story of a giant redwood tree that lies in ruins on the slopes of Pike's Peak. Naturalists say that it stood for four hundred years; during that time it had been struck by lightning fourteen times, and innumerable avalanches and storms had hit it. It survived them all. In the end, however, it fell because an army of tiny beetles ate their way through the bark and destroyed it.

Most of us start each year with big dreams and lofty goals, but we often get sabotaged by little things—interruptions, telephones, telephoning people who aren't home, unexpected house guests, loss of electrical power when we are making final preparations for a dinner party, cars that won't start, children who quarrel, fellow workers who don't do what they promise, houses that need cleaning. James W. Moore, in his book *You Can Get Bitter or Better* (Abingdon Press, 1989), quotes a New York doctor who says that civilization's three major killers are not heart disease, cancer, and accidents. Instead, they are calendars, telephones, and clocks—the tyranny of the fast lane. Dr. Moore says that there is an office building in Detroit nicknamed Ulcer Alley.

Pressure debilitates us, and so do resentment, envy, and jealousy. Oscar Wilde told the story of the devil who came upon a group of people tormenting a holy man. They had tempted him with wine, food, beautiful women, money, worldly pleasures, but he had resisted all of them with poise and serenity. The devil said to the tempters, "Your methods are too crude, too obvious. Allow me." Then the devil whispered to the holy man, "Have you heard the news? Your brother has just been made bishop of Alexandria." Immediately a malignant scowl of jealousy clouded the holy man's formerly serene face. Jealousy, resentment, envy, gnaw at us and devastate us from within.

How can we cope with little things that destroy us? It seems to me that Jesus beautifully integrated interruptions and pressures into his life by doing the following things:

First, he never lost sight of his purpose, but kept it steadfastly before him. This enabled him to simplify his lifestyle and to travel lightly.

Second, he understood that persons, not things, are of ultimate value. How we need to understand this in the families of America.

Third, he did one thing at a time without being compulsive, hurried, or harried. You can't imagine him running around Galilee in a panic, pushing people aside as he hurried on to his next appointment. In the Sermon on the Mount, he said, "Don't be anxious about tomorrow." Just take it one day at a time, one thing at a time, one step at a time.

Above all, he trusted God for the future. In the parable of the sower, he suggests that it is our job to sow the seed and to cultivate it to the very best of our ability, and then to trust God to bring the harvest. It is marvelous to remember that we don't have to run the universe. God is still in charge!

14

Steps to Spiritual Fitness

JUST ABOUT EVERYBODY I KNOW IS INTO PHYSICAL FITNESS. THEY ARE walking, jogging, riding bikes, doing aerobics, or pumping iron at home or in a gym. That's great news, because in the 1970s we were in danger of becoming a nation of couch potatoes, glued to our television sets. Today, the components of physical fitness—nutritional eating, exercise, adequate rest, and relaxation—have been incorporated into the lifestyles of millions of people.

Centuries ago, Paul realized the importance of this when he told the Corinthians, who were well known for their indulgence and debauchery, that their bodies were the temples of God (1 Cor. 6:19).

How sad it is to see our spirits and souls, the eternal part of us, given so little consideration or care. On a flight from Cleveland to Atlanta, I sat beside a woman whose beautifully sculpted body encased a broken and bitter spirit. It was obvious that she was a woman of wealth and considerable sophistication, as she placed her Louis Vuitton carry-on in the overhead racks, tossed her Gucci bag onto her seat, and removed the jacket of her Armani suit.

Here is a well-traveled woman who probably has interesting stories to share, I thought as I mentally took out paper and pen. How wrong I was! Here was a well-toned and beautifully draped body, but her spirit had atrophied. There was no joy, enthusiasm, or hope in her words, only despair and bitterness. It occurred to me that unless we care for the whole person—mental, spiritual, as well as physical—we can expect to become shallow, even hollow, half selves.

I have found the following disciplines helpful to renew a barren or joyless spirit:

First, spend thirty minutes each day in stillness—quiet reading, thought, meditation, prayer. Our conscious minds become so filled with schedules, plans, and anxieties that creative thoughts don't emerge. As I heard a speaker describe it once: "Ships don't come in on troubled waters."

It was the prophet Isaiah who wrote, "In quietness and confidence shall be your strength" (Isa. 30:15). If we don't make time for stillness, we are destined for shallow living. As I read the biographies of great people who have made a difference in the world, over and over I discover that their actions come from a center of inner peace and calm.

Second, try giving yourself away. Give smiles, compliments, warm handshakes, time, money, and random deeds of kindness with no thought of return. The philosophy of "me-ism," so prevalent in our culture, creates brash, selfish individuals who are insensitive to the needs of others. Jesus recognized this in his paradoxical teaching that if we want to save our life we have to lose it in service (Mark 8:35). Some people give up something for Lent—parties, rich desserts—but I like to think of taking on some form of service in love and gratitude.

Third, practice joy every day. In a fast-paced world filled with problems, it is easy to focus on the negatives. Instead, count your blessings, look for joy, remember the joyful times of your life, and plan to bring some form of joy each day into the life of another. Remember also that joy is the fruit of God's spirit dwelling within us.

Fourth, spend some time with children. Their spontaneity, enthusiasm, and joy in living will jump-start a weary spirit. If you aren't near children, remember the fun parts of your life as a child. It's children's trust and openness that must have caused Jesus to say, "Except ye . . . become as little children, ye shall not enter the kingdom of heaven" (Matt. 18:3).

Finally, renew your spirit through regular worship, through listening to great music, and through reading inspirational books. The way to find joy and purpose in living, I believe, is to practice fitness for the part of us that will live eternally. I challenge you to have a spiritual springtime in whatever time of the year you are living.

15

Searching for the Truth?

I SLIPPED INTO MY FAVORITE EASY CHAIR TO WATCH THE EVENING news. Though I have come to expect the daily report of a certain amount of violence and unpleasant news, I was in no way prepared for what I saw. Before the eyes of millions lay the dead bodies of thirty-nine neatly dressed and appropriately covered men and women. These persons were found on March 27, 1997, in a large, contemporary home in the upscale community of El Rancho, California. They were between the ages of twenty-six and seventy.

According to the reports, they were members of the Heaven's Gate cult and believed that only by taking their physical lives could their spirits be transformed and transported in a UFO which, they were convinced, followed in the wake of the Hale-Bopp Comet. How could such supposedly intelligent, college-educated people be so gullible?

As I searched for the answer to those questions, my mind recalled a similar but more horrendous scene. The year was 1978, and in Jonestown, Guyana, nine hundred persons drank Kool-Aid laced with cyanide at the crazed bidding of Jim Jones, leader of People's Temple cult. Though we were shocked by this tragedy, most of us had become somewhat immune because of the violence, protests, and riots of the late sixties and early seventies.

The reason we were catapulted into more anxious concern about the Heaven's Gate cult was that they were on the World Wide Web. Thousands of persons were having this bizarre gospel piped directly and simultaneously into their brains through the Internet. According to *FaithLink,* a publication of Cokesbury, in the United States there are currently more than five hundred registered cults involving more than thirty million people. (Incidentally, the word *cult* comes from the Latin word *cultus,* meaning "worship" or "a set of religious beliefs or rituals.")

Some anti-cult groups have concluded that the most dangerous are not those dealing with the occult, such as Satan's Own. The reason is that there are relatively few of such groups and their appeal is not wide. Instead, anti-cult groups say, the most populous cults, and potentially the most dangerous for our culture, are those that deviate from Judeo-Christian doctrine and provide counterfeit spirituality.

According to George Gallup, more Americans are on a search for spiritual truth now than at any other time during his years of surveying the American public. Religious demographer George Barna reports that almost eight out of ten Americans (85 percent of the population) consider themselves Christian, yet sixty-five million adults and twenty-five million young people do not attend an established church service in any given six-month period. He believes that this spiritual search, combined with no established faith community, has made the people vulnerable to such cults where they find acceptance, purpose, and accountability.

Interestingly, whereas in the late 1960s cult members were mainly in the eighteen to thirty-five age group, today there are increasing numbers of middle-age to senior adults. This latter age group makes up the growing number of devotees of the New Age movement. While not technically listed as a cult (it has no overall organization or leader, though several gurus), it is a kind of eclectic grab bag of spiritual goods. Based on Hindu beliefs, it negates many beliefs of the Judeo-Christian faith, which has defined the American culture.

Among the practices and beliefs incorporated in the New Age movement are reincarnation, channeling, meditation, spiritual guides, astrology, alchemy, and numerology. Critics of the movement have called it "paganism repackaged"—a thinly disguised pre-Christian cult, though some of the terminology has been updated. For example, a medium is now called a "channel." Other critics have expressed concern about its focus on the self rather than on helping others, or on relieving human misery.

Seated in my easy chair that evening of March 27, I felt very uneasy in my spirit. It occurred to me that if we are to go "beyond Heaven's Gate," it means that as people of faith we need to do three things. We need to know with certainty what we believe, so that we won't be swayed by "every wind of philosophy that blows." We need to be more actively committed to a faith community; and most important, we need to daily live our faith in every aspect of our lives.

16

Aging Gracefully?

MARGARET SKEETE OF RADFORD, VIRGINIA, LIVED TO BE ONE HUNdred and thirteen years old and was included in the *Guinness Book of Records*. I first met her in 1982 when I spoke at a women's meeting in that town. In the business session preceding my speech, a participant asked for a matter of special privilege; she wanted to honor one of the two hundred women present.

When the honoree stood, I thought, *What a lovely-looking elderly woman.* She was petite and immaculately groomed. Her coralcolored suit softened and enlivened her face. Her gray hair was beautifully coifed.

During the presentation, the presenter expressed gratitude for Margaret Skeete's active participation in church and community groups; for her happy, optimistic attitude; for her caring concern for others; and for her delightful sense of humor. Then came the shocker: Margaret Skeete was one hundred and four years old then.

It was hard to believe what I was hearing. This was no "little old lady in tennis shoes." I learned later that she always wore high heels, never wore slacks, still made her own clothes (all in pretty colors—she didn't like black or navy), put on makeup every morning, and was always well-groomed.

In checking on her background, I learned that she grew up in Texas and was a dressmaker in Houston. Her first husband died after two years of marriage. A number of years later she married a rancher, Reen T. Skeete, and they moved to San Angelo, Texas. There were two children, a son and a daughter. Following the death of her second husband, Margaret moved to Radford to live with her daughter.

As I think of this remarkable woman and others who have lived beyond the biblical "three score and ten years," I wonder what is the secret of their longevity. More important, what is the secret of aging gracefully? Nobody wants to be a cantankerous, complaining old person. Such persons create unhappiness for themselves, and torment for close relatives and friends.

My observation of Margaret and others who have aged gracefully is that they have several things in common. First, they take good care of themselves. They eat nutritious foods, exercise, and take vitamins. In other words, they stay active and keep those muscles moving.

Second, they think right. There is no hardening of attitudes for these people. They are interested in what is going on now in the world. They are not obsessed with the past or unduly concerned about the future. They are in touch with today.

Third, they are disciplined. Like Margaret, they provide structure for their lives. They get out of bed each day, get dressed, and follow through on a plan. A friend of mine told me that her mother taught piano when she was in her eighties. One day her mother said, "If I give in to my feelings, I'd stay in bed today, but I won't." That's discipline.

Fourth, they have chosen to be happy and live with hope. By the time you have lived to be eighty or ninety or one hundred, you have had some hard experiences in life. You can choose to be happy "in spite of." This kind of choice makes for personal serenity and pleasant interpersonal relationships.

Finally, the people who age gracefully have learned to "trust in the Lord with all [their] hearts; and lean not unto [their] own understanding" (Prov. 3:5). As all of us live longer, perhaps our prayer should be not only for more years for our life, but also for more life for our years.

17

Does Your Anchor Hold?

IT WAS A PERFECT DAY FOR BOATING—OVERCAST, BUT NOT RAINING; warm, but not humid; a northeasterly breeze's light chop to the water made it challenging, but not dangerous. In addition, it was a Monday morning, so my husband and I virtually had Chickamauga Lake to ourselves.

The boat belongs to our son and his family, and they encourage us to use it weekly. It is a delightful experience. We enjoyed cruising the lake, which in the summer is surrounded by lush vegetation and visible mountains in the background. It was so quiet that morning, we could hear the birds sing and see the fish jump. After a busy, hectic weekend, it was like an oasis for dry and thirsty spirits. I kept thinking of the words of the youth camp song: "God who touches earth with beauty, make my heart anew . . . recreate me" (Mary S. Edgar, "God Who Touches Earth with Beauty").

Later we found a cove, anchored the boat, had a picnic, swam, and sunned. Memories popped into our minds about other boating experiences we had when our boys were young. My husband's brother owned a cabin cruiser that slept six persons. He and his family liked to go one way on the Tennessee River or the Kentucky and Ohio Rivers, and our family made the return trip. Our first trip down the Tennessee River was when the boys were seven and eight. The night before, we weighed anchor, slept on the boat, and encouraged the boys to go to sleep immediately because, we said, 'We'll be leaving at the crack of dawn." About 2:00 A.M., Rick tapped his dad on the shoulder and asked, "Has it cracked yet?" Sleepily, my husband inquired, "Has what cracked?" The excited eight-year-old replied, "Dawn. Has it cracked? I haven't heard it." It is a story we have told for years in our family.

Another trip we made was down the Kentucky River and up the Ohio River. We had anchored just outside Coney Island in Cincinnati so that we could enjoy an afternoon and evening at the amusement park. It was late when we returned, so we decided to sleep on the boat rather than go to the marina. The boat was tied to a tree on the shore and anchored off the stern. The Ohio River had been at flood stage, but during the night the waters began to recede rather rapidly. At about 3:00 A.M., my husband awakened to find our heads pointed downward and our feet pointed upward. Quickly he awoke the three of us to help cast off before the boat was beached. Debris from the storm had collected around the boat and anchor, and though we could pull the anchor up from the mud, we couldn't free it from the heavy debris. Finally, we had to cut the rope and leave the anchor at the bottom of the river, and seek the marina.

On that Monday as we talked about boats and anchors, I thought about how problems and difficulties cut people loose from their moorings and set them adrift on life's sea. In such cases—death of a loved one, serious illness, divorce, financial reverses, loss of a job, rejection and betrayal, and other disappointments—many people find their boats drifting, with no anchor that holds. Does your anchor hold in such a situation?

Priscilla J. Owens posed that question and answered it in the old hymn "We Have an Anchor":

> Will your anchor hold in the storms of life,
> When the clouds unfold their wings of strife?
> When the strong tides lift, and the cables strain,
> Will your anchor drift, or firm remain?
>
> We have an anchor that keeps the soul
> Steadfast and sure while the billows roll,
> Fastened to the rock which cannot move,
> Grounded firm and deep in the Savior's love.

18

Words Can Hurt or Heal

ONE SPRING I HAD A BAD CASE OF LARYNGITIS. THAT IS NOT A GOOD experience for anyone, but for someone who talks a lot, it's an abomination. I believe the Chinese proverb: "God gave us two ears and one mouth because he wants us to listen twice as much as we talk." Still, I don't like it when I can't talk at all.

When we have laryngitis, we begin to understand the power of words and just how wonderful the gift of speech really is. Several years ago, I read a report from the telephone company which suggested that the average American uses 10,182 words in an average day. When I read that, I thought, *I have an aunt who uses that many words in one telephone conversation.*

As people created in the image of God, we have a responsibility to use our words to fulfill God's purposes. An artist was once asked, "When is a painting finished?" He replied, "When it fulfills the intent of the artist."

When is a life complete? I'm convinced that it's when that life fulfills the intent of the Creator. Those purposes are fulfilled not only through our deeds, but through our words as well.

As children we learned and sometimes believed "sticks and stones can break my bones, but words can never hurt me." Words, however, can hurt—or they can heal. Words are like barriers that separate people from each other, or like bridges that bring them together. Words of destructive criticism are barrier words. They put people down, causing them to lose heart and feel rejected. This doesn't mean that we shouldn't guide or correct, or that we shouldn't offer constructive criticism. It does mean that we should deal with the deed and not attack the person.

Words of appreciation are bridge words. Sincere appreciation builds people up, encourages them, motivates them. Who is the person who has influenced your life most for good? Is it someone who criticized you constantly? My guess is that it is someone who recognized your faults, but through encouragement and appreciation helped you to become more than you were. I have a pet theory that no one in my family—and no one in your family—should receive more appreciation outside the home than they receive in the home. We are to be encouragers to each other.

Words of prejudice are barrier words, causing people to feel inferior because of their clothes, their nationality, their color, or their economic situation. Words of acceptance can free us to perform at our highest levels, and release our creativity. If we are accepted, we don't have to spend all of our energies trying to prove ourselves.

Words of gloom and despair are destructive barriers. When I went for my annual physical last year, I sat in the waiting room near a rather large, middle-aged woman who greeted me with "Hello. How are you?" I replied, "I'm fine. How are you?" I opened myself up for that one, because she told me exactly how she was. In fact, she gave me an organ recital of every organ in her body. Without asking, I learned all the gory details of her four operations, as well as a recital of her weekly aches and pains. I had come into the waiting room feeling chipper and cheery, but by the time I entered the examining room, I was filled with gloom and despair. This was the result of hearing words.

Words of hope are bridge words. It's wonderful to know that we are never alone in this world. God is with us. He is with us in sunshine and rain, in happy times and sad, in sickness and in death, and most of all, in the life to come. If we ever fully grasp the significance of this, we can pass on our hope and joy to others.

The words of the poet R. L. Sharpe summarizes the importance of this:

> Isn't it strange
> That princes and kings,
> And clowns that caper
> In sawdust rings,
> And common people
> Like you and me
> Are builders for eternity?

Each is given a bag of tools,
A shapeless mass,
A book of rules;
And each must make—
Ere life is flown—
A stumbling block
Or a stepping stone.
   ("A Bag of Tools")

19

Ready for Bad News?

IT WAS TO BE A ROUTINE GALL BLADDER SURGERY ON MAY 3, 1988. AS Louis sat in the hospital waiting room, he fully expected to have his good friend Tom, the surgeon, walk up to him and say, "Louis, Belton came through fine. She will be back in her room shortly, and you may see her then."

But the script turned out to be very different. Louis knew something was wrong when Tom asked him to step into the family room for a private conversation. Then the bomb fell! In calm, measured tones the surgeon said, "Louis, we found something we had not anticipated. Belton has a rare form of cancer of the bile duct, and it has metastasized in the liver. It is inoperable. There is no known cure and little satisfactory treatment." In answer to Louis's question, Tom replied, "She probably has about three months to live."

Professionally, Louis had been a research chemist for a company in Tennessee. He was accustomed to dealing with scientific facts. From his wife's surgeon that morning, he heard some hard, cold, scientific facts. But Louis is also a committed Christian, and when the doctor asked if he could call someone to be with him, Louis knew that he needed spiritual strength.

He asked for Sparky, a young engineer who was a member of Louis and Belton's prayer group. Sparky and his wife, Gail, arrived to take Louis home, where other members of their prayer group awaited them. That night, Louis found the strength he needed for the ordeal ahead. A part of the ordeal was accompanying Tom to break the news to Belton the following day.

"She didn't flinch," said Louis. "I have never seen anyone take bad news with more courage and dignity. Throughout her entire illness, she never showed resentment or asked 'why me?' At times there was terrific pain, great fatigue, and much discomfort, but she never—never—was angry, depressed, or bitter."

According to Louis, during the three and a half months of her illness, she maintained her good spirit and sense of humor. One night when she couldn't sleep, she composed the following:

Ode to Louis

When it comes to a back rub, you are an old pro.
You prepare my favorite dishes that taste "just so."
You help me with my bath with such love and care.
But why, oh why, can't you backcomb my hair?

Also during a sleepless night she wrote:

Some die so young, before they have a chance to live and enjoy the wonders of the world. Others live too long—past their time of usefulness, outliving all their friends and leaving no one to miss and mourn their leaving.

If I could choose, this is the time I would die—at the crest of a wave while I am still needed and useful, surrounded by those I love. I count myself so very blessed. Through travel, I've been able to see much of the world's beauty and grandeur, and my friends have included an interesting variety of people. Also, I have been blessed with a talent that seems to fulfill a need in others.

But in examining the different facets of my life, what stands out are the times when the love of Christ in me could flow to my family and friends. Those rare moments when his love reigns supreme between me and another made all the other experiences of my life seem so very insignificant.

If I could leave a message to the heart of the world, it would be this: Never let an opportunity go by to express God's love to another. We are the only vehicles through which his love may be expressed. Do not take this love for granted. It is the "pearl of great price." Our Lord valued it enough to die for it, so that it could become real for us.

During her stay in an Augusta, Georgia, hospital, Belton was taken from the hospital to the home of their son, a physician. There she had a massive hemorrhage. She broke out in a cold sweat, a strange expression came over her face, her neck stiffened, and her eyes rolled back. Momentarily she died. When they were able to revive her, she said, "Please leave me alone; let me be."

Later she told her husband that it was so beautiful there. It seemed right and very peaceful. There was an unfamiliar, but pleasant, fragrance. She felt the presence of Christ very strongly and knew that he wanted her there. She also told Louis that if the experience occurred again, she did not want to be revived.

That experience helped prepare Louis for her death, and enabled him to release her with peace in his heart. Before she died, she had outlined a lesson that she wanted presented in her adult Sunday school class. Louis gave the message some three months later. In it, Belton reminded her friends of the little girl who was asked what she liked most about the church. Quickly the little girl replied, "The benediction." Belton had written: "This is what we should like best about life—the benediction, the establishment of the kingdom of God."

Then, through Louis, she said, "Live as fully as you can each day, remembering that God uses human vessels as instruments through which he manifests himself."

Thanks be to God for this beautiful witness from a talented, dynamic, and gallant woman.

20

Said Your Good-byes?

REFUSING TO GET OUT OF BED, AND SAYING THAT SHE DIDN'T WANT TO go on without Kirk, Martha Rhien wailed, "I didn't even get to say good-bye." She was speaking to my friend Herb, a former Army chaplain. Herb had come to tell Martha and her four children—ages six, nine, eleven, and fourteen—that TWA's call had definitely confirmed what they had feared: Kirk Rhien was indeed listed on the manifest of TWA's jumbo jet Flight 800.

Martha's heart seemed to shatter with Herb's words. She fairly screamed, "I'm never going to get out of this bed. I don't want to go on living." Herb listed empathetically as she poured out her anger and pain. She spoke of the irony of her husband missing his scheduled flight at 6:00 P.M. because his business meeting in New York had run overtime and his driver came even later to pick him up. This necessitated Kirk's taking the ill-fated flight so that he could keep a Thursday appointment in Paris.

Forty-two-year-old Kirk had left their summer home on Lake Erie only the day before. The large house overlooking the lake had been in his family since he was a little boy. It held special memories of his childhood, and now provided happy summer experiences for his growing family. For the past several years Kirk had been an organizer for the community's elaborate Fourth of July parade. So, he, Martha, their four children, and their entourage (cook, maid, nanny, and so forth) always moved to the summer place by mid-June. From time to time Kirk would commute to New York or Connecticut for business meetings. It was such a meeting and the resultant need to be in Paris that caused Kirk to be on the TWA Flight 800.

Herb listened for a long time to Martha's understandable pain. He affirmed her feeling but spoke firmly, "You must get out of bed. You must take a shower, dress, and provide strength for your children." She replied, "They love their nanny, and she can do that for them." He was insistent. "You're wrong there, Martha; only you as their mother can give them that kind of strength."

Being a person of strong Christian faith, and knowing in her heart that Herb was right, Martha pulled herself together and not only comforted her children, but was on hand to greet family and friends as they arrived. The hotel in which my husband and I were staying was only a half block from the Rhien home, and we could see Martha as she and her family ate dinner on their patio. It was a solemn group, but there was some quiet laughter as they obviously remembered happier times.

Though my husband and I left the resort early the next morning, Herb called to say that Kirk's body had not been found, but that Martha was on Long Island with the families of the other victims. She planned memorial services in their church in Connecticut, and in Kirk's parents' church in Ohio.

Martha, of course, is devastated and will continue to grieve, but her inner strength comes from her sure knowledge that her husband, as a Christian, is alive in a new dimension of life, and that she and her children will see him again.

That brief but unforgettable contact with a family caught in tragedy reminded me that life is fragile, that tragedy can strike at any time, that only our faith can hold us steady, and that we should never put a period where God put a comma. After all, life does not end in six feet of earth or on the floor of the Atlantic Ocean.

21

Is God's Grace Sufficient?

"HOW CAN I GO ON WITH LIFE AFTER LOSING MY HUSBAND? WE WERE so close, and were almost always together." These were the words of a woman who talked with me at a women's retreat I led on St. Simon's Island, Georgia. Her husband had been dead two and a half years, but she was still in a state of shock.

My mind went back to a telephone interview I had with Wilma Dykeman Stokely just one month after her husband's death in 1977. "Wilma Dykeman Stokely is a thoroughbred," I said to my husband after an early morning interview with this tall, stately woman from Tennessee. Despite the fact that she was leaving town shortly after we talked, there was no trace of self-pity or hurry in her well-modulated voice. In fact, her voice had the same bell-like quality I remembered from our first meeting ten years earlier. At that time she and her husband were lecturing on the campus of Tennessee Wesleyan College, where my husband was serving as president. I felt drawn to her like a bee to honey. Intelligent, articulate, urbane, and witty, this well-known author communicated with verve and excitement.

In the sudden death of her "perceptive coauthor, wisest counselor, mentor, and love," she was passing through some deep waters. *Will the grace of God be as evident in her life in the dark days as in the beautiful, sun-filled days?* I wondered. After talking with her, I decided that God's grace was even more evident as she walked through this personal tragedy.

She recalled for me the days of their courtship and marriage: "I was picking flowers in my mother's garden in Asheville, North Carolina, on that August Sunday morning when Thomas Wolfe's sister and her husband drove into our yard with two young men— the Stokely brothers from Newport, Tennessee. One of them wore a white shirt, open at the collar and with rolled-up sleeves, against which his smooth skin was a golden tan, and his eyes were the clear blue of the sea or sky. Before that day was finished, he had asked me if I liked books, and the woods, and the final question—Beethoven. Two weeks later I canceled my career in New York, and in October we were married. I believe there never was a couple more destined for each other.

"Very few people knew the true dimensions of James' life. In a world where outer appearances are judged as reality, he invested more and more of his time in inner riches. In a time when vigor is considered best, and power seems the prize worth any sacrifice, he cherished the fragile spirit, the delicate creativity that flows from an eternal power. In a period where the loud and self-proclaimed receive the world's awards, he was quiet and self-forgetful."

I was mesmerized as Wilma continued. "People sometimes ask if he were disconcerted by my writing, by my career. How little they knew him! He had no identity crisis, no need to narrow anyone else's life to enhance his own. Indeed, one of the purposes of his life seemed to be to make sure that everyone—no matter what race or sex, social status or creed—not only had opportunity, but encouragement to be the best they could be.

"A week ago he left on one of the few trips we have not taken together, but he is not wholly away—and I am not wholly here. We are still together."

Not only are they together, but also Wilma is allowing the light of God's grace and love to shine through her personality, through her writing, and through her lectures in the eternal here and now. She is indeed one of God's thoroughbreds.

Perhaps one of the greatest tests any of us will endure on this earth is the death of a loved one. When such an experience came to me in the death of our twenty-year-old son, I learned two things. First, you can't go through this period without hurting. There is no such thing as love without pain as well as joy. Second, in life's traumas, God's grace *is* sufficient. Lean on it! You, too, will become one of God's thoroughbreds.

22

Journeying Out of Darkness

"WHEN I AWAKENED EACH MORNING, I FELT THAT I WAS GOING TO BE able to function, but by the time I walked halfway across the room, a dark cloud seemed to envelope me." These were the words of Mary as she described her long years of dealing with depression. Her exciting recovery began seven years ago with a Christian conversion experience and has been accelerated through the support of her family and Christian friends. She pays special tribute to the help provided by her pastor. His counsel, guidance, and encouragement have enabled her to grow toward emotional and spiritual maturity.

In retrospect, Mary recognizes that she had evidences of depression even as a child—lots of "blue days" and very low self-esteem. Her depression is believed to be a combination of difficult life experiences and an inherited genetic weakness. Her mother suffered the same disability and was hospitalized from the time Mary was nine months old until she was fifteen. Since her parents were divorced, Mary went to live with her widowed grandmother.

A good woman, her grandmother was not warm or affectionate, and never attended Mary's school activities. Without affirmation at home, Mary often felt lonely, discouraged, and lacked self-confidence. At that point, she didn't even know that God loved her.

When her mother returned after fifteen years of hospitalization, her withdrawn and robotlike appearance frightened Mary. It's small wonder that Mary left home and was married at sixteen. From the beginning it was a bad marriage. Five years and two children later, she was divorced from an alcoholic husband.

One day when she was at work and the children were being kept by a relative, her former husband came and took the children. Young, naive, and not knowledgeable about her legal rights, Mary was intimidated by his threats of what would happen if she tried to get her children back. She became withdrawn, bitter, depressed, and miserable.

Later she married a wonderfully supportive man, with whom she will soon celebrate a thirty-fourth wedding anniversary. They moved to Florida, where she attended beauty school and worked as a hairdresser. It was in Florida that their son was born. Eventually she was able to regain custody of her other two children.

Though she had regular bouts of depression, it wasn't until she returned to Chattanooga in 1975 that depression hit her with a vengeance. As she described it, it was then that the "dark cloud" enveloped her. She simply couldn't function. "I cried out to God for help, but never repented of my bitterness nor sought his guidance," she said. "Suicide seemed the only way out."

Fortunately, she was wise enough not to attempt that, but instead to admit herself to a psychiatric hospital. She is grateful to the doctors and staff for insights she gained, but the medication had detrimental side effects. For one thing, she gained an enormous amount of weight—from 125 to 203 pounds, and she reacted to life like a zombie. She felt trapped.

Seven years ago, a daughter-in-law told Mary that Mary needed to experience God in her life, and invited her to go to church. It was there that she found acceptance and support, and where she had an evangelical conversion. Mary released her resentment and bitterness, and she received the "peace that passes understanding."

She has been off all medications for four years, but her complete freedom from depression has come gradually. "When I couldn't sleep at night and battled the demons of fear and anxiety, the Holy Spirit healed my mind through giving me poetry," she said. Her poetry is beautifully expressive and would help anyone who is battling depression.

One Sunday morning, her pastor gave each member of his congregation a dollar bill and asked that they use their talents to multiply the money for the building of a much needed sanctuary for their growing congregation. Mary felt that her God-given talent was writing poetry, but she felt that no one would buy her poems. Still, she copied them, put them together in a bound notebook, and from their sale earned about three hundred dollars for the church project.

Hers is a wonderful story of victory over depression, a journey out of darkness, through her faith in Christ. She gives special thanks to a supportive husband and the encouragement of her pastor. Her message to others suffering from depression is this: "Hold on; don't give up. There is hope."

23

Don't Put Off Until Tomorrow

"NEVER PUT OFF TILL TOMORROW WHAT YOU CAN DO TODAY."

My no-nonsense mother said that at least once daily during my growing-up years. She said it about household chores, homework, writing thank-you notes, and calling a friend to apologize. It was so indelibly imprinted in my mind that I have had to work hard to develop any shred of flexibility or spontaneity. Yet it is a lesson well worth learning. Some people sabotage their lives through procrastination.

Actually, the quotation was written by Phillip Dormer Stranhope, fourth Earl of Chesterfield. He was a brilliant British statesman and man of letters who certainly lived by his own philosophy. He died in 1773 at the age of seventy-nine, after one of the busiest careers in history. His full quotation is this: "Know the true value of time; snatch, seize, and enjoy every moment of it. No idleness, no laziness, no procrastination. Never put off till tomorrow what you can do today."

In life, as in baseball, you can avoid making an out by getting a hit, or by never going to bat. Too many people sit on the sidelines of life because they are afraid of failure. Several years ago I met a young artist who had done some excellent work in oils and water colors, yet he never would allow his work to be shown or sold. He was always working to improve it. His perfectionism, according to his mother, stems from fear of rejection. As a result, he is like the man in Jesus' parable of the talents. There was the one who buried his talent, and thus never glorified God by making a contribution to the world.

Strangely enough, another reason for procrastination is fear of success. Some people—and especially women—are afraid to liberate all their God-given talents for fear that it may adversely affect their marriages, causing spouses to be resentful, envious, or competitive. Both men and women don't succeed as often as they might because they are afraid of moving ahead of their peers and risking their rejection.

The truly great and transformational leaders have glorified God by using all their talents to the fullest, but balancing that with sensitivity to the feelings of others and a genuine desire and willingness to help others succeed.

A third reason for procrastination, I have observed, is resistance to authority. If we don't like to take orders, chafe under authority, or have unhappy memories of an authoritarian parent or teacher, we will find ways to procrastinate. People who are constantly late, or who often forget to do things they are asked to do, or who become obstructionists in business sessions, are usually hostile to authority.

If we wish to overcome our tendency to procrastinate, we need to do these things: First, accept the fact that procrastination is a personality cancer that kills our opportunities for effective living. Second, we need to face honestly our reason for procrastination. Are we afraid of failure, of rejection, of success? Are we resistant to authority?

Third, face our fears. Ask, "What is the worst that could possibly happen in this situation?" When we know we can deal with the worst that can happen we are willing to take risks, to try new things. We can follow Emerson's advice: "Do the thing you fear and the death of fear is certain."

There are times when we need professional help to deal with fears and hostilities. In some cases it means the healing of early memories, or help in overriding early programming. Sometimes we need a detailed step-by-step action plan to overcome deeply embedded fears.

If we feel we can do this on our own, then we need to heed William James' advice to "act as if." He said that actions affect emotions as much as emotions affect actions. Most people feel and then act the way they feel. If they feel lousy, they act lousy. If they feel cheerful, they act cheerful. The late Dr. James, Harvard sociologist and psychologist, says that we ought to decide how we want to live our lives and then act as if we already live that way. The feelings will follow. For example, ask a man who won a purple heart in battle if he were frightened. He will likely say, "Of course I was afraid, but I acted courageously, and the feelings of courage followed."

If this seems superficial, remember that Shakespeare said, "Assume a virtue until you have it." It was John Wesley who said to his young preachers: "Preach faith until you have it, then you will preach it because you have it."

In my own life, I have found that certain biblical quotations, when used as affirmations, are a source of tremendous help when I am fearful: "I can do all things through Christ who strengthens me" (Phil. 4:11); and "If God be for us, who can be against us?" (Rom. 8:33). When I was beginning to speak publicly, it was the combination of using affirmation—of acting as if I were confident—and of determination that allowed me to overcome my fear of public speaking.

Remember, the God who created us with talents and individual potential is not glorified when we bury our talents or hide them behind procrastination. So, never put off until tomorrow what you can do today.

24

Believe in Yourself

MY DAY HAD BEEN CROWDED AND STRESSFUL—A DISHWASHER THAT wasn't working, so that the simple chore of dishwashing took twice as much time! The tedious job of correcting a manuscript was lengthened by constant interruptions. The bright spot of my day was watching my granddaughter, a middle school student, participate in a track meet late in the afternoon. The excitement of that event was dampened when parents and grandparents had to sit huddled under umbrellas and raincoats in the driving rain.

I was in no mood for an upbeat interview with speaker and best-selling author Jack Canfield, but he was expecting my call at 5:30 P.M. So, wet and hungry, I placed the call to a man whose book *Chicken Soup for the Soul* (Health Communications, 1993) has been number one on the *New York Times* best-seller list. In less than five minutes of conversation with this man, whose books and speeches have helped hundreds of people believe in themselves, I had forgotten the problems of the day, and felt energized enough to conquer the world.

Jack Canfield is a powerful motivator. Married, with three children, he is perhaps best known for his pioneer work in the importance of self-esteem, and serves as chairman of the board of the Foundation for Self-Esteem.

The need that each of us has for believing in ourselves and having strong self-esteem was most evident to him twenty years ago when he was a teacher in an inner-city school. He noticed that the children were extremely verbal on the playground, but became shy and reticent in the classroom. He began a study of what blocks the use of the potential of the human mind.

The program, which he developed to enable people to live happy, more fulfilling lives, has been taught in varying formats to educators, Fortune 500 executives, and religious and government leaders on three continents. From reading his books and listening to his tapes, I am convinced that every person can profit from his ten specific steps for becoming a happier, more fulfilled, growing-and-achieving person.

First, move forward by completing the past. Second, use positive self-talk to quiet the inner critics of doubt and perfectionism. Third, acknowledge your personal and professional strengths. Fourth, clarify your vision of the future before attempting to get there. Fifth, after clarifying the vision, set specific goals and objectives.

The sixth step is the number one secret of successful persons, including star athletes: See yourself as succeeding—whether it is playing a golf game, giving a speech, or conducting a business meeting. Afterward, affirm your success.

Seventh, take action—now. Give up the "if onlys," and just do it. Eighth, respond positively to feedback. It is through constructive criticism that we can see ourselves most clearly and can grow. Ninth, persevere. Just keep on keeping on. Don't stop short of the goal. Tenth, celebrate every success along the way.

His theory of "E + R = O" means "Event plus Response will equal Outcome." It is Jack Canfield's belief that what happens to us is not nearly as important as how we react to what happens. In addition, he suggests that if we are to reach our peak performance, we need to surround ourselves with nurturing personalities instead of toxic ones.

One thing about the interview especially impressed me. When I said, "You have accomplished so much in your life. What are you most proud of?" without a moment's hesitation, he replied, "Our three children." He is both a family man and a person of strong religious faith. I commend his "Ten Steps."

25

When in the Eye
of the Storm

DO YOU FEEL LIKE YOU ARE LIVING IN THE MIDDLE OF A HURRICANE? Are problems, difficulties, disappointments, deadlines, and tensions turning your world upside down? Are you blown away by the winds of change in your life?

If so, consider the formula developed by Wilma after living through Hurricane Andrew in Homestead, Florida, August 24, 1992. Her formula: Prepare for storms; in the midst of them, don't panic, but stay calm, pray, and trust God.

I met Wilma when she was chair of a women's conference in Florida where I was speaking. Wilma is a well-organized, competent, and positive leader. I never would have guessed that she had been through such a nightmarish experience except that one of her friends told me.

Wilma and her husband had built a beautiful new home on a ten-acre lime grove, owned jointly with one of their sons. Their son and his wife were living with their young son in a garage apartment on the property while their home was being built.

During the week before the storm, a mutual friend was at Warner Robbins Air Force Base in Macon, Georgia. When he heard news of the approaching storm, he called Wilma and insisted that she and the family head north immediately. His formula for storms had always been, "Board up the windows and head out."

Wilma's philosophy, on the other hand, was "Board up the windows and stay put." Her rationale was that when the storm ended, you were there to clean up quickly and repair, keeping damage at a minimum. On August 24, Wilma, her daughter and son-in-law were comfortably situated in the new house. They watched a movie on the VCR, popped popcorn, and had a fun evening.

By midnight, waves of rain beat against the house, and the new roof began to leak. When the full fury of Andrew hit, their plan was to go to a hall closet that had reinforced walls on three sides. By

2:00 A.M., they had lost electricity, and the winds and rains were creating a deafening roar. They decided to go to the quietest room of the house, a middle bedroom, and try to rest before the height of the storm really hit.

They were barely in the room, however, when kitchen windows were blown out. When they attempted to open the bedroom door and go to the hall closet, they were struck by glass and flying debris. Retreating to the bedroom, they recalled and followed storm instructions from a TV anchor man: "Put box springs up to the window, with a chest of drawers in front of them. Push the bed against the door to keep it closed. Sit on the floor and hold a mattress over you."

Then they heard it—it was like the sound of a freight train coming right through the middle of their house. For what seemed to be hours, they stayed on the floor, which now had three inches of water.

Suddenly there was a slight lull, and they decided it must be the eye of the storm. Once again they tried to get to the hall closet, but now there was a two- by six-foot board from a window frame blocking the door. They were barely back on the bedroom floor when the freight train returned. For five hours they clung to each other, trying to hold on to the mattress amid driving rain and wind.

Wilma told me that during those frantic hours, the presence of God was very real to them. "I am claustrophobic, but he took care of that," she said. "Not once did I panic. We sang hymns and praise songs. We quoted favorite passages of Scripture. We prayed. Despite the fact that we knew we might die, we felt we could say with Paul: 'Whether I live or die, I am the Lord's.'"

Even so, she thought with sadness about her husband returning to a destroyed home and a dead family.

Fortunately, they were not among the missing or dead when the storm finally ended. At 7:00 A.M., Wilma's son and his family walked over from their garage apartment into what was left of the house. They hugged each other and joined in prayers of thanksgiving, rejoicing that they were all alive.

Since the telephone lines were down, Wilma's husband had to drive down Tuesday morning from Macon through the disaster zone of South Florida, not knowing what he would find in Homestead.

What a wonderful reunion they had as they stood amid their rubble! They focused not on what they had lost, but on what they had left. After all, the house could be rebuilt and the lime grove could be replanted. Most important, they were all alive.

As they walked around the house and grounds, Wilma found her Lenox figure of Jesus holding two little children. He had his arms around them. The figurine was blown about twenty feet, off the mantle in the living room, onto the hard Mexican tile floor of the dining room. Yet there was not a crack or nick in it. For her, it was symbolic that as children of God, no matter how far we are flung or how hard we land, Christ is with us, holding us and loving us.

If or when you are in a storm in your life, prepare as much as you can, don't panic, stay calm, pray, and trust God.

26

Your Choice: Bitter or Better

"YOU HAVE A CHOICE. YOU CAN BE BITTER OR BETTER." THOSE ARE THE words I heard in the Columbus airport. One woman was saying them to another; the two were seated in back of me, and I couldn't see them. Because of the noise, I could catch only bits and pieces of the conversation, but I did gather that the woman receiving the advice was in the midst of an unwanted divorce.

It was only when we stood to board the plane that I got a good look at both women. The one giving the advice looked as if she might be in her early forties. She was slender, of medium height, had short, well-coifed black hair, and violet eyes that seemed to dance when she smiled.

The woman receiving the advice looked very young—perhaps in her early twenties. She, too, was attractive—tall, blonde, with brown eyes. But there was no smile on her face. It was obvious that she had been crying; she had a distraught, frightened look.

I certainly would like to know what prompted the older woman to give such succinct and wise advice, I thought as I made my way to my seat. Although it wasn't a prayer, I did feel that it was providential that the forty-two-year-old woman was seated beside me. Her name was Norma, and she was from Oklahoma. After we indulged in a bit of small talk about the weather and our sections of the country, I thanked her for the advice which I had heard her give the young woman. Then I asked what had prompted it. She looked at me carefully as if to decide whether or not she could trust me with her story. Suddenly she took a deep breath and began.

She told me that she had been married for ten years to her college sweetheart. He was handsome and successful as a sales representative for a large company. They had two beautiful children, ages six and four. Jim traveled each week, but when he was home she felt that they had a happy marriage. In retrospect, she realizes that everything centered around Jim's interests and that he was never very attentive to the children. She had dismissed this as his being tired from travel.

As a result, she was devastated when he told her that he had been having an affair with her best friend and that he wanted a divorce. She felt as if she were in the middle of a bad dream. She felt angry, betrayed, bitter. She cried, and retaliated with angry words. She begged Jim to go with her to a marriage counselor. He refused. Her emotions were on a roller coaster, from lows of suicidal thoughts to highs of denying that anything was wrong.

When Jim actually moved out, she plummeted into depression. She lost interest in everything—her appearance, her financial future (the only positive thing she said about Jim was that he had been fair in this regard), even the children. Her usual self-confidence disappeared, her interest in and concern for others vanished, and her natural ability to plan and organize was in disarray. Friends and family became deeply concerned about her health and mental stability.

The one positive thing she continued was her lifelong habit of attending and taking her children to Sunday school and worship at a large Protestant church. For months she went out of pure habit, but she was so detached that she heard nothing that was being said. Then one Sunday the young minister in her church began his sermon with this challenge: "The choice is yours. You can be bitter or better." These words pierced her mind with the speed of a bullet and the sharpness of an arrow.

She sat up and listened as he talked about how we all have storms, tragedies, or circumstances over which we have little or no control. But he told his congregation that we each have the choice of how we will react to these experiences. Then he drew graphic pictures of those who choose bitterness: They will be filled with resentment, anger, depression, and unhappiness. On the other hand, he said, we can allow God to walk with us through these hard experiences, and allow Him to heal our hurts. We can choose to learn from the difficult experiences as we move into the future.

When he spoke of how in our bitterness we lose our concern for others, she became aware of her children's needs. After all, in the divorce, she had lost a husband, but they had lost a dad whom they adored. In fact, if she continued to live in depression, they would lose both parents.

That Sunday morning in church, she saw clearly that God had created her as an individual, as a person of worth, a person loved and redeemed by Christ. She was not just an extension of her husband. Though her husband had broken her heart, he could not (unless she allowed it) destroy her spirit. He could not take away her self-identity. That was God-given, but she must reclaim it.

The words spoken by Paul to the Christians at Philippi began to cascade through her mind like a waterfall. "I can do all things through Christ who strengthens me" (Phil. 4:13 NKJV). She walked out of the church that morning empowered to look toward the future rather than the past.

That Sunday of her awakening had happened three years ago when I talked to her. Today she is a better person, not a bitter one. That doesn't mean the way has been easy. There have been times of loneliness, times when rearing two children alone have left her fatigued and uncertain. But she said she has never again felt desolate or deserted. She knows that God is with her.

I learned also that she has returned to her teaching profession; is enjoying her family, friends, and especially her children; and that she is an active participant in the singles ministry in her church.

This is the story Norma had shared with the young woman at the airport; the young woman had just begun her trip in the "valley of the shadows." At our next stop, when the two women embraced and said good-bye to each other, it seemed to me that the newly divorced woman was walking a little straighter. Maybe she had already made the decision to become better instead of bitter.

27

Are All Things Possible?

PENNY BELIEVES IN MIRACLES. IN FACT, SHE IS CERTAIN THAT SHE received one. It started on February 18, 1996, when she attended the early worship service at her church. She went alone that day, since her husband, Doug, was out of town on a business trip and their children were visiting her husband's parents. In the bulletin was an announcement that the minister would be taking a group to a prayer conference in Jerusalem in April.

Suddenly Penny experienced a strong feeling that she was to go on that trip. It was far more than just a desire to go, though she had thought from time to time that she would like to walk where Jesus walked. Her concern about terrorism in Israel and her fear of flying caused her to put even the slight desire on the back burner. In addition, there were other obstacles: Her passport had been misplaced; the Israel trip came during her wedding anniversary and her daughter's sixth birthday (events she wouldn't think of missing); there was no one to keep her children; and there was no money for the trip, since she and her husband had just built a new home. So she dismissed the idea.

Yet the following Sunday when the minister asked the congregation to be silent and see what God might be saying to them individually, the message that came to her was loud and clear—"Go to Israel." On the way home from church, Penny asked her husband to ask God to speak to him about what she felt led to do. The following week, her prayer group prayed that she would know God's will with certainty and that she would receive some confirmation. The first confirmation came when her husband gave his blessing for the trip, if they could work through the obstacles.

Bit by bit, answers seemed to fall into place like a jigsaw puzzle. A friend who would be on spring break from her teaching position at the university would keep the children while Doug was at work. Penny's passport was returned to her in seven days rather than the usual three to five weeks. Gifts of money began to arrive from friends—four hundred dollars in all, but far from the amount needed for the trip. Even so, Penny saw it as a confirmation that she had heard the message correctly and was indeed to go to the Holy Land. She felt that her job was to be prepared and to stand firm in faith.

She cooked and froze enough food for her family during her ten-day absence. She washed and ironed and packed her clothes in readiness for the trip, and she never wavered in her faith. Even when obstacles arose and things didn't seem to come together as fast as she needed them to, Penny had an inner peace about the situation. Penny's mother told her that she would believe with her and would hold in her mind the picture of Penny walking up the steps of the airplane.

Saturday morning arrived, and Doug took Penny to the airport to join other members of the church who were going on the trip. The difference was that they had round-trip tickets to Tel Aviv and paid reservations for the entire two weeks. Penny had only an unshakable faith. Actually, a Christian friend had given her his ticket to New York, but in trying to use it, she discovered that his signature was needed. Now, every door seemed to be closing as the group boarded the flight to New York.

In the meantime, her parents were attending the party of a grandchild in a nearby city. While seated at a restaurant amid the raucous noise of a preschooler's birthday celebration, Penny's mother had a sudden revelation. It was an unexpected message, but it was as clear as if someone had spoken to her audibly. Turning to her husband, she said, "Bobby, I have just had a revelation that we are the ones who are supposed to provide the money for Penny's trip." Penny's father agreed, and they began a wild ride to the Nashville airport, stopping only long enough to pick up money from an automated bank teller.

They arrived just minutes before Penny was to step onto a private plane belonging to contemporary Christian singer and composer Michael W. Smith. Most Christian young adults would give a right arm just to meet Michael W. Smith. To ride with him and his entourage to New York was the ultimate experience. To Penny, it was just another neat piece of God's miracle.

In New York she was invited to stay in the home of a former minister and his family while she waited for a seat to open up on an international flight. She, who had never been abroad and who had a fear of flying, walked alone onto the Monday flight with perfect calmness. When the church group arrived at the prayer conference at a hotel in Jerusalem on Tuesday, Penny was there to greet them. There was great celebration!

Already Penny knows several reasons why God wanted her at that conference, she expects to discover more in the months ahead. One of the most obvious was to increase her faith and teach her to trust God's promises.

As I reflected on this experience, I remembered the story told in Matthew 9:29 of the blind men who asked Jesus to give them the miracle of sight. Jesus asked, "Do you believe that I am able to do this?" They replied, "Yes, Lord, we do believe," and immediately their eyes were opened. When Jesus restored their sight, he made a statement that seems applicable to Penny Everett: "According to your faith, be it unto you."

28

Does Your Face Say "Yes" or "No"?

WHAT IS YOUR FACE SAYING TO THOSE AROUND YOU? WHETHER WE like it or not, our faces express our thoughts and feelings as clearly as our words—sometimes, more clearly. So, without planning for it, walk toward a full-length mirror today, and see what your face is saying.

What is the climate you create? We carry our own weather with us wherever we are—at home, at work, at school, at the church. Is your climate sunny and pleasant, or gray and stormy? Personal auras are created by personal appearance (including facial expressions), relational skills, and commitments.

It was in 1965 when I began to understand how faces have an impact on other people. My husband and I went to Russia soon after that country was beginning to be open to tourists. We were there in October, and already it was bitter cold. Men and women, looking stoic, trudged through the streets with their coats drawn tightly around them. It was a chilling experience.

Once as we walked through Red Square in Moscow, I commented to my husband, "Nobody here is smiling, and East Berliners weren't smiling, either."

"Well, they don't have much to smile about," he replied.

Since then, I have often thought about our faces. I realized that I had never really looked at faces of people whom I see daily in the streets here at home. "After all," I reasoned, "we live in a democracy in which there is freedom of speech, freedom of religion, opportunities for education, for leisure, for free enterprise, and for free elections. I'm sure that I will see smiles in the U.S.A. because we have much to smile about."

When we landed in New York and I began to look at faces, I was stunned to discover that so many of them looked grim, unsmiling, unhappy. This was true not only in the large metropolitan area, but in small-town America—even Southern small-town America. Because I have known many of the people behind the faces I have observed, I know that they are basically not unhappy people. Then, what happened to their faces? It looked as if they were saying to themselves the age-old adage: "My face, I don't mind it, for I am behind it; the fellow in front gets the jar." In actuality, most of these people were reflecting preoccupation, hurry, stress, frustration, or a combination of these. Intent on what they were doing, had done, and will do, they failed to realize how their negative feelings created a climate around them.

This was certainly true for me when I was den mother for a Cub Scout group when our sons were young. One day I took the Cub Scouts out to the airport to see a display of Confederate money. While a guide was explaining the display, I paid little attention to the children. Instead, I was thinking of all that I had to do in preparation for a women's meeting at our home that evening. I hadn't finished cleaning, hadn't prepared the dessert, so I was totally preoccupied.

When we returned to the car, one of the boys asked, "Mrs. Mohney, are you mad?"

"Oh no, I'm not mad," I replied. "Why did you think that?"

"I didn't, but one of the boys did, and I told him that you probably had eaten something that upset your stomach."

Since that day, I have tried to check my face each morning before leaving the house to be sure that I don't look like I have an upset stomach!

Think of teachers who, even inadvertently, have grim, angry faces. Think of the impact they have on small children, or on high-risk children, or even on teenagers who are already torn apart by family stresses. Think of the impact of preoccupied, uninterested faces on people who are going through the trauma of divorce or the death of a loved one. Think of the effect of the harsh, judgmental faces of some Christians on people who have lost their way and need some sign of hope and meaning—some good word from God.

Abraham Lincoln is reported to have told of fording a stream on horseback when a stranger on the bank asked to ride across with him. Lincoln graciously granted the request, but said to the man, "I notice that you let five men go across ahead of us. Why didn't you ask them for a ride?"

The man replied, "Some people's faces say 'yes,' and some people's faces say 'no.'"

In his book entitled *Abundant Living* (Abingdon Press, 1990), E. Stanley Jones says, "We are not responsible for the faces we were born with, but we are responsible for the faces we die with." He explained how our dominant thoughts and beliefs become written indelibly on our faces.

In the stresses of today's world, however, how can we have faces that exude warmth and caring even when we feel little more than frustration? Is it phony to work on it? Absolutely not! Down deep, most of us want to affirm others rather than tear them down. We want to give hope rather than despair, and we want to make a difference for good rather than for evil.

In my own life, I have found a simple threefold formula that seems to work for me: gratitude, focus, and remembering. Each morning when I awaken and before I get out of bed, I try to condition my mind with gratitude for all the blessings I have in my life. On the rare occasions when I oversleep and have to skip the conditioning, I am irritable with others and impatient with myself.

Second, in a fifteen- to thirty-minute quiet time, I focus on who I am and whose I am. I focus also on the goodness and power of God, and the fact that nothing can happen in life that God and I together can't handle. This energizes and empowers me.

Third, just before I leave the house, I think a series of happy thoughts, and remember some of the pleasant experiences of the day before. All this seems to "set my sails," and when I do these things, my face usually says "yes" instead of "no" to others.

29

Appreciating Each Season of Life

WHEN THE GROUND WAS COVERED WITH SNOW AND ICE, AND IT WAS bitterly cold outside, I found myself repeating a line from Shelley's "Ode to the West Wind": "If winter comes, can spring be far behind?" Most of the time when I have used this quotation, I have felt as if I were whistling in the dark, or at the very least, hoping for something that might not occur soon.

But on this particular day, despite a 30-degree temperature, I saw jonquils and crocuses popping up in our yard—a sure sign that spring was just around the corner. As I observed this phenomenon of nature, I thought how fortunate I am to live in an area where the seasons are so distinct. Each has its own uniqueness—its special beauty. God has created great variety in this marvelous world, and we have the privilege of enjoying and appreciating each in its own season.

The same is true of the seasons of life. As the book of Ecclesiastes tells us, "To every thing there is a season, and a time to every purpose under the heaven: A time to be born, and a time to die; a time to plant, and a time to pluck up that which is planted" (Eccles. 3:1-2).

In the springtime of our lives, when we are young, everything seems alive with possibilities and promise. We never think of dying in this gloriously alive time of our lives. How fortunate are the youth who are not only trained to use their minds and keep their bodies fit, but also are nurtured by strong family ties and an unshakable faith in God. These are the ones who have built strong foundations for their houses of life. Every child deserves this right and the opportunity to enjoy the season of springtime—to make happy memories.

The summer of life is young adulthood, with its challenges of continuing education, choosing a vocation, establishing a family, and of making faith a major part of the fabric of life. It is a lively, exciting, busy season. If strongly held values are incorporated into friendships, family relationships, vocations, and avocations, this can be one of the happiest of all seasons.

The autumn of life is often referred to as "prime time." The people who have toughed out the earlier seasons can enjoy the harvest during these years. It is usually at this time that their children go away to college or into the workforce. If the children are happily established in their own lives, parents reap a good harvest of contentment and joy. If the autumn people have become wisely matched with their own vocations, they can make their strongest contributions vocationally and through church and community. This is when the leaves of gold will begin to emerge.

Then comes the winter of life. Some people dread this time from their earliest years. It is true that our physical bodies begin to slow down and often become frail during this season. It is also true that we might not make the strong contributions we made in the springtime and summer of our lives. But our winter has its own special beauty. It is in this season that we have time to show more concern for others. We can write notes of appreciation, make friendly telephone calls to express our concern, and pray for our friends and neighbors.

In the winter of life, we can share some of the wisdom we have accumulated (but only when asked). We can fully develop the qualities we deeply want in our lives—such as loving-kindness, graciousness, compassion, thoughtfulness, intelligent concern, and a sense of humor. In this season, we can curl up with the Bible and prepare for our final battle with pain. We will do this with the knowledge that the God who has been with us in life will not desert us in death. He has, as Jesus promised, "Gone to prepare a place for us." So, in the words of Robert Browning: "Come, grow old along with me. The best is yet to be."

30

They Have Said Yes to Life

THIS WILL BE A QUIET, SEDATE, LESS ENERGETIC GROUP THAN THE AUDIENCES to which I usually speak. These were my thoughts when my plane landed in Brunswick, Georgia. I was en route to St. Simon's Island, where I was to be one of the speakers at a large conference for senior adults.

The beautiful retreat facilities could have been an advertisement for Sustecal. The whole place was "jiving." One group was doing line dancing, another was playing bridge, another was jogging, and another was seated in easy chairs, with members telling stories of funny experiences from past conferences. Certainly this was no "quiet, sedate, less energetic" group. There was no gloom and doom here.

Suddenly it occurred to me that my original thought was an old stereotype of senior adults. The ones I know today are fully alive after fifty-five. They are more physically fit than the last generation of seniors. As a result, they like to travel, grow mentally and spiritually, socialize, have fun, and serve.

My responsibility during the four days we were together was to be the Bible study leader. Here again, they were not passive participants. At each session, the senior adults brought their Bibles, having studied the assigned chapters, and participated freely in the discussions. Wishing to convey the idea that God has a purpose for all of us as long as we live, I chose Bible characters who served God effectively, especially in their golden years. Since they have something to say to us today, regardless of our age, check yourself as I list a few of the points.

First, consider Abraham and Sarah, who, surrounded by family and friends, were called by God to leave that comfortable, secure spot and go into an unknown land when Abraham was seventy-five and Sarah was sixty-five. They pulled themselves out of pleasant ruts and made their finest contributions after "retirement years."

How many of us settle too easily into the ruts of our lives? I've even heard of some people who don't like to sleep in a bed other than their own, or eat foreign or unusual foods. Pretty soon we paint ourselves into a corner—comfortable, but boring. When we give in to this temptation, we miss some of life's greatest adventures, and we certainly turn a deaf ear to God's call to new areas of service.

Second, we talked about the life of Jacob and all his vicissitudes, many of them caused by his own manipulative deceit. We learned that God doesn't save us from the consequences of our actions, but can use what he doesn't choose. Despite Jacob's mistakes and failures, he sought God's direction and power, and God made him the leader of the Israelite nation. Often we, too, are discouraged by failures and stupid mistakes. But in the words of the contemporary song written by Gloria Gaither: "All I had to offer Him was brokenness and strife, but He made something beautiful of my life" ("Something Beautiful").

Then we looked at Moses, who had the gigantic task of leading the children of Israel out of bondage in Egypt and to the doorway of the promised land. He had to take off his shoes when he stood on holy ground in front of the burning bush.

It seems to me that we often don't realize when we are on holy ground. Unfortunately we often are so focused on the next rung of the career ladder that we fail to appreciate where we are now or what we have achieved. We think so much about getting a larger house, or what we will do when the children are older, that we fail to realize that right now we are standing on holy ground. To be alive is to stand on holy ground, to have an honest job and live with people we love is to stand on holy ground, to live in a country where we can practice our faith freely is to stand on holy ground.

Yes, the senior adults at the conference were not what I expected. They were so much more! They have said yes to life. So they are growing, caring, serving persons; they are blessing others and making a difference in their world.

31

Flying Around in Heaven

"IT JUST CAN'T SNOW ON THIS VALENTINE'S DAY. PLEASE GOD, DON'T let Marsha be disappointed." That was my prayer as I lay in my bedroom at home suffering from an upper respiratory infection, including laryngitis. There was nowhere I wanted more to be the next day than in Marsha Toomey's hospital room when she graduated with a master's degree in business. But even if my temperature had been normal, I knew that my young friend was vulnerable to every germ, and I didn't dare go. So, I stayed home and prayed that she wouldn't have to sustain another disappointment.

It did snow on that February 14, yet my prayer was answered. My beautiful young friend, Marsha, who was terminally ill with cancer, was not disappointed on her twenty-third birthday.

Despite the constant television reminder of hazardous driving conditions, and the weatherman's plea to stay inside unless absolutely necessary, the assistant dean of the university's college of business administration kept his promise to Marsha to present her MBA degree in her hospital room on her birthday. He not only made the trip from Knoxville to Kingsport, when a lesser man might have felt justified in giving up on the project, but he also brought along two of Marsha's friends and classmates who had traveled with her on the university's European study tour.

In addition, he arrived at the hospital wearing snowboots and full graduation regalia, and carrying a mortar board for Marsha. According to her mother (my friend), Barbara Goodlett, that graduation ceremony was a sublime experience for everyone present. She told me that Marsha, wearing her mortar board, listened intently as the assistant dean went through the entire graduation ceremony (complete with ritual parts from her classmates), received her diploma, shook the assistant dean's hand and accepted congratulations, and transferred the tassel on her cap.

In her delightful book *Twenty-three Valentines from Marsha,* (self-published, 1993), Barbara tells the story of her brave daughter. Concerning the graduation ceremony, Barbara tells of an interesting aside during the solemn event: Barbara's father whispered to a friend, "Now who is that man in the robe again?" The friend replied: "I think it is God." Certainly the caring, courageous act of the educator had heavenly results in the life of the graduate. She immediately exuded new energy and joy.

There is never a Valentine's Day that I don't remember the privilege of friendship with a young woman who lived life with zest and joy despite recurring battles with cancer since she was twelve years of age. In fact, during my own months of chemotherapy, it was the memory of Marsha's joyful courage that sometimes kept me going. She died on October 1, 1986, and whenever I wear the pearls she left me, I remember our friendship with great gratitude.

From the time we moved to Kingsport in 1981, I knew Marsha as one of the young people in our church. You couldn't not know her. In the first place, she was strikingly beautiful—tall, willowy, with long and shiny blonde hair that bounced, and a smile that lit up her face. In addition, she had an irrepressible joy that expressed itself in an interest in everything, including people of all ages; in helping others as an expression of her faith; and in loving to share ideas.

I began to know her well when she came home from Clemson University for summer vacation. Marsha, as well as many other students, worked on projects at the church; the students were in and out of my office frequently.

But it was after her cancer recurred in 1985, while she was a graduate student at the University of Tennessee, that my friendship with Marsha deepened. Following surgery at Duke, she returned to Kingsport for more chemotherapy treatments. On the days she was feeling well she would often pop into my office and say, "Well, what needs doing today?" I would sometimes reply, "Filing. You can file all the things on that table while I write notes."

In between our work we would talk about everything from fashion (she looked smashing even as she got thinner, and wore turbans when her hair came out again) to faith. She wanted to know what I believed about God and Jesus and heaven. We explored each of these through her penetrating questions.

Our discussions were deep but never sad. Her sense of humor spiced every conversation, and often regaled me with laughter. Once I observed her irrepressible joy and thought that Jesus must have been speaking directly to Marsha when he said, "These things have I spoken unto you, that my joy might remain in you, and that your joy might be full" (John 15:11). She personified what Nehemiah said: "The joy of the Lord is [my] strength" (Neh. 8:10).

There was one conversation I shall never forget. I think of it every year on her Valentine birthday and whenever I see a butterfly. One day when we returned to the church from having lunch, several monarch butterflies were flitting hither and yon amid the flowers at the back of the church.

Inside my office, before we settled down to work, she said, "Nell, I think death will be like a butterfly. We'll leave our sick and tired bodies behind like an old cocoon, and we'll emerge as a butterfly unencumbered by time and space and limitations. God has arranged a neat plan."

Then laughingly, she said, "When I die, and you see a butterfly, you remember that I am flying all around heaven happy and free."

Yes, Marsha, I do remember, and especially on your birthday. I believe you are not only happy, but as usual, you're making others happy as well.

32

Still Singing?

"Whoosh!" It was like the sound of a giant Dustbuster. Marian knew exactly what had happened. She had decided to take a short-cut to cleaning the bird cage that housed her favorite canary, named Chippie. Having a busy schedule that day, she decided to clean the cage with the vacuum cleaner. Shortening the process even further, Marian took off the attachment and used the full hose to remove debris from the cage.

Suddenly the telephone rang. She turned to answer it when she heard the loud "whoosh." There was no doubt about it—Chippie had been sucked into the vacuum cleaner bag. Quickly she hung up the receiver, opened the bag, and found Chippie—still alive but filthy.

She went to the bathroom, turned on the faucet full force, and stuck Chippie beneath it. A few minutes later, he was clean but shivering. Seeing the hair dryer on the counter, she turned it on "high" and quickly had Chippie dry, warm, and back in the cage. The entire procedure had taken only a few minutes. Days later, someone asked, "How's Chippie?"

"Well, he seems to be okay, except that he doesn't sing anymore. He just sits and stares out into the room."

When I read that short news story several years ago, it occurred to me that our lives in the current culture are analogous to Chippie's. Changes are happening with frightening rapidity. The cumulative effects are enough to traumatize us—drive-by shootings, teenagers killing parents, accelerated use of drugs, the breakdown of the family, neglect and abuse of children and the elderly, rise of pornography.

Sometimes I feel that decent, law-abiding citizens seem almost dazed. We have become grim and intense, and no longer have a song in our hearts. What will start the music playing again?

Obviously, we need to rediscover our spiritual roots and deepen them. For me, this is the Christian faith. When I feel weighted down by personal cares and the woes of the world, Jesus puts a song back into my heart. He reminds me that I am loved and cared for, and that I'm not the manager of the universe. I realize that I can't do everything to make the world a better place, but I can do something. And what I can do, I will do with the help of God.

With this perspective comes a peace that allows me to live calmly in the midst of chaos, and puts a song back into my heart. His love motivates me to deepen my roots through worship, Bible study, prayer, and service, and to allow my spirit to catch up with my body.

Once during a terrible storm, two giant oak trees came uprooted and crashed into our garage, with both of our cars in it. When a tree surgeon came to assess the damage, he said that the roots of the trees were not deep enough to withstand the winds of hurricane strength. Our lives will be buffeted about by storms of many varieties. Even the accumulation of daily pressures requires spiritual roots. But when the big crises occur—death of a loved one, divorce, loss of a job, financial reverses, serious illness, a child on drugs, and so forth—they require spiritual roots that go deep in our souls.

In addition to the usual spiritual discoveries of prayer, worship, and study, I believe we deepen and strengthen our spiritual roots when we seek God's will and become obedient to it. He needs all of us at whatever age or in whatever situation we find ourselves. If we seek God's purposes, he will reveal them.

Since our retirement, God has opened so many doors of service for my husband and me that we sometimes feel we don't have time to catch our breath. It is exciting, but tiring. One Saturday night, after having spoken to a large group in Baldwin, Kansas, I was awaiting a flight at the Kansas City airport.

I was fatigued, still had a long flight ahead of me before my 11:20 P.M. arrival in Chattanooga, and needed to study in order to teach Sunday school the next morning.

Good grief, I thought. *I'm too old for this.* I thought retirement meant sitting around and complaining about your health, eating chocolates, and watching television.

Suddenly God brought to my remembrance a plaque which hangs

on the wall of the Red Bird Mission in Kentucky. The plaque reads: "One evidence of the presence of God in your life is when you look down and find your feet where you didn't expect them to be."

I definitely had not expected in retirement to find my feet in Kansas City on a Saturday night. I could only smile and say, "I received your message, Lord. You have given me a song, and I'll keep on singing."

Confirmation of that experience came. I told my Sunday school class the story of Chippie and of my experience in the airport. One of the members sent me an adorable plastic bird in a cage. Every time you touch the cage, the bird sings. The card read: "Don't stop singing."

That's my advice to you: "Don't stop singing."

33

Inner Beauty Shines

SHE IS A TALL BLONDE MODEL WHOSE LOVELY FACE AND FIGURE ARE seen in newspapers almost weekly. She is also the model and spokesperson for Porsche cars at their shows across the country. But Myra Brown is not just another pretty face. Her beauty is inner as well as outer. In addition, God has given her a dream, which she is pursuing with vigor.

One day she and I had lunch together, and she told me of her dream. It is to help girls ages six to eighteen learn to believe in themselves as worthy creations of God. Her motivation for this comes from her own background.

For whatever reason, Myra grew up not feeling good about herself. Maybe it was because she was always taller than her peers. In her teen years, she was already five feet nine and a half inches tall. She was teasingly called the "Jolly Green Giant."

"Not only that, but I was skinny, studious, homely, and never felt included," she added. While it is hard to believe that Myra could ever have been homely, it was the way she saw herself.

Or maybe it was because she was born with a sensitive nature that internalized teasing, criticism, and lack of affirmation. As a teenager, she felt ungainly, ugly, and like a passive observer rather than an active participant in life. As a result, she became somewhat retiring, unsure of herself, and totally without confidence.

Two things have been especially helpful in restoring her self-acceptance and confidence. First, when she entered a modeling career, she found a new level of competence. As she succeeded, more and more doors opened to her, such as becoming spokesperson for Porsche Automobile Company.

Second, she made a new commitment to spiritual values. Always a believing and practicing Christian, she nevertheless was traumatized by the tragic death of her sister, and felt the need for a more trusting relationship with Christ. Observing the disciplines of prayer, Bible study, and seeking God's will has enabled her to face some old patterns of fear and insecurity. She realizes her worth comes not from what she has done, but from what God has done for us through Christ.

That day as she sat across the table from me, she looked radiant in her newfound confidence, and she shared her dream of helping girls and young women develop good self-esteem and responsibility for their own happiness. She does this through a modeling camp that she instituted three years ago; it's entitled "Inner Beauty Shines."

In addition to teaching things such as good posture, how to stand and sit, and how to perform on the runway, her main emphasis is on inner beauty. "Modeling is only a tool to accomplish my main purpose—that of instilling principles for happy and productive living." The program includes developing self-esteem through such things as respecting your body, the importance of good nutrition, exercise, and behavior.

"Respect your body and expect to be treated with respect," she tells her students. In a day when sexual promiscuity is rampant, Myra advocates respecting your body, and sex only within the marriage relationship. She helps the girls understand the dangers of promiscuity, including AIDS and unwanted pregnancies.

Speaking briefly about the death of her sister, Myra tells her students that tragedy, grief, and disappointment may come to each of us and that faith in God is the only thing that will hold us steady.

Focusing on the good rather than the bad, and thinking positively are two strong emphases. "If we can help young people control their thinking, focus on possibilities rather than problems, and build on the positives, these become a habitual response to life," she said.

The camps run for four days from 10:30 in the morning to 3:30 in the afternoon. There are both beginner and advanced camps for girls ages six through eleven and for girls ages twelve through eighteen. Almost 100 percent of those attending the beginner camps return for the advance sessions. At the close of each camp, there is a program and fashion show to which the girls invite their friends and parents.

While many of her campers later become models, Myra's major concern is to help young women become all that God created them to be. She hopes they will become positive, productive human beings who practice fitness in every area of their lives—physically, mentally, emotionally, and spiritually.

She never wants them to feel that they are victims, but rather that they have something special to contribute to the world. She wants them to believe in themselves, to be the best they can be, and to have inner beauty.

Go for it, Myra! Yours is a wonderful dream.

34

Caught in a Storm?

DO YOU EVER FEEL THAT YOU HAVE SO MANY STRESSES AND TRAUMAS that you are living in the eye of the storm? In a seminar I conducted in Myrtle Beach, South Carolina, one of the class members told of being in Hurricane Andrew. He lived in an outlying area north of Miami. While residents had been told to prepare and batten down for the storm, it was anticipated that the eye of the storm would be south of them.

As the storm approached, it veered slightly so that the fury of the storm headed straight for their community. It was too late to evacuate. Besides, all roads headed north were filled bumper-to-bumper with cars of "snowbirds" and natives trying to get out.

Jim and his family quickly gathered some food, a flashlight, and a portable radio, and headed for the basement of their home. Already the wind was blowing at high velocity, and the rain was torrential. It was an eerie feeling having his family—he, his wife, three children, and a cocker spaniel—huddled together waiting for the catastrophe. It happened less than ten minutes later.

First, they heard windows breaking with explosive power as the glass was literally sucked out of the house, then a violent shaking as the house was being pulled away from its foundation. They were terrified, convinced that all of them would be killed. Yet, in a few moments, there was a scary silence except for the sound of the wind and rain, which now was coming through the basement ceiling. Jim said that before trying to get out, they huddled even closer and gave God thanks that they were still alive. That in itself gave them perspective to face the destruction of their home.

There is an analogy here for all of us as we face emotional, mental, and spiritual storms. Just as people along the coast need to expect hurricanes at certain seasons, and just as the people in California know there will be earthquakes, we need to know that our lives will include rough water, not just smooth sailing. In John 16:33, Jesus reminded us that "in the world you will have tribulation; but be of good cheer, I have overcome the world" (NKJV).

It always surprises me when people ask, "Why me?" "Why did this bad thing happen to me?" Perhaps a more appropriate question would be, "Why not me?" "As a member of the human race, or even as a Christian, why should I be exempt?" In this world we will have storms and tribulations.

Second, we can be as prepared as possible. Jim had bought food, flashlights, a generator, rain gear, and a portable radio for his family. Knowing that storms will come, we need to have our priorities in order, with faith and family right at the top of the list. We need to remember that material possessions, no matter how valuable, can be replaced, but human life cannot.

Third, we need always to give thanks for what we have left, and begin rebuilding. While there has to be a time for experiencing grief, processing the trauma, and readjusting our plans, we must lean into the future rather than bogging down in self-pity and living with the "if onlys."

Fourth, Jim said that their network of friends became a powerful ally during this time of suffering. They supported and helped each other in their grief and their rebuilding. We have just come through a time that emphasized independence and "me-ism." How much wiser we will be to emphasize our interdependence and the value of true friendship. Friendship is one of life's greatest joys and treasures, and will be a strong support when we have to live in the eye of the storm.

Jim commented also on the wonderful help they received from complete strangers. "While we were all saddened that some plundering occurred, most of us were overjoyed at the outpouring of compassion and help. Tangible help was sent in the form of money, blankets, medicine, equipment. Also, teams of people from teenagers to senior adults came from all over the United States and several foreign countries to help with the rebuilding."

In addition to government help, the National Red Cross, and other agencies, help came from ordinary citizens who still believe that "we are our brother's keeper."

It was the late Pitirim Sorokin, professor at Harvard University, who said that in time of cataclysmic events, people are polarized into two categories—the saints and the sinners. It is the former group that reaches out in compassion and helps. The latter is interested only in satisfying selfish desires and in profiting from another's misfortune. Dr. Sorokin suggests that the difference in these two stems from their basic value systems. One is based on spiritual values, and the other on sensory values.

Perhaps there is another group who may believe in spiritual values, but do not act on them. They have grown apathetic and unmotivated. During Hurricane Andrew, these were the people who sat on the sidelines, watched the happenings on television, and took no action. Only the people who act out of their spiritual value system can really make a difference for good in our world.

Finally, just as Jim's family was protected with the solid foundation of their home, so our lives will stand eternally when they are based on a firm belief, and trust in God's purposes as exemplified through Jesus. It was Jesus who told us in Matthew 7:24-27 that we should build our houses of life on the rock, so when the winds blow and the storms come, our houses will stand.

35

Climbing Your Mountain?

GOING INTO A SEMINAR LED BY STAN COTTRELL IS LIKE WALKING INTO a highly charged magnetic field. This man has more energy and enthusiasm in his little finger than most of us have in our entire bodies. The atmosphere is electric when you walk into the room with him.

It's more than energy and enthusiasm, it's his humor as well. It explodes like firecrackers throughout the seminar from beginning to end. It certainly keeps you awake. It also relaxes you and makes it easy to listen. I went into the seminar having just returned from a speaking engagement where the travel delays were stressful. I was physically exhausted; in addition, I had a sinus headache. I came out of the seminar energized and excited.

But there was far more to the seminar than humor and enthusiasm. There was pathos. In a forthright but lighthearted manner, Stan told of some of his life's struggles. He was born in the backwoods of Kentucky—"Gobbler's Knob, which is near Dry Creek"—to well-intentioned, but uneducated, parents, he said. His father was a big man physically—six feet four inches tall, 240 pounds, and expected his sons to be the same. He wanted them to be hunters as he was, or to play basketball for the University of Kentucky and make lots of money.

When Stan turned out to be skinny and short of stature (at age thirteen he was only four feet seven inches tall and weighed 70 pounds), his dad was sure there was something wrong with him. Not only did he call his son "Runt," "Puny," and some other unflattering names, but once a month he made Stan take a worm pill, the kind he gave to his prize hunting dogs. Regularly he also had his son eat lard—to "grease his joints." While we recognize this as child abuse, Stan came through this without any hatred or bitterness. This internationally known long-distance runner did bring tears to our eyes when he told of running the Great Wall of China and realizing, though his dad had been dead for five years, that he was still trying to win his father's approval.

In my opinion, it was his mother who saved him from bitterness and led him to a strong Christian faith. When Stan would run to his mother, crying, and ask, "Why doesn't Dad love me?" she would reply, "He loves you, but he just can't show it." Then she always added, "I love you and God loves you. He has something special for you to do. You are not only special, but you are 'specialer.'" Incidentally, when Stan speaks to young people, he always reminds them of their uniqueness and of the fact that they are "specialer." He and his children have made a movie entitled, "You are Specialer."

As this belief became ingrained in him, he was able to take every setback and use it as a stepping stone. Stan had started his running career when he chased rabbits and cows on the farm, but it came into focus when he was age twelve. He won first place in a race at the county fair. In his senior year at high school he was offered a small scholarship to Western Kentucky University, where they were beginning a track program. His principal said, "Don't do it, boy. Nobody from Gobbler's Knob ever goes to college. You will only make a fool of yourself." A statement like that only seemed to make Stan more determined to prove that he could do it. He not only received recognition for his running ability in college, but since that time has logged more than 135,000 miles of ultra-distance running. His remarkable accomplishments include a 3,500-mile, 80-day run through Europe; a 3,103-mile, 48-day transamerica run; and a 2,125-mile run across China.

Stan is also the founder of Friendship Sports, a nonprofit organization that promotes the spirit of friendship among the nations through sporting events. He held a highly publicized "Friendship Run" through Vietnam and planned a "Friendship Run" through the Soviet Union, Cuba, North Korea, and the Middle East.

Another example of his turning a setback into a stepping stone is an experience that happened in a speech class at Western Kentucky University. His professor told him that she should give him an F in the class because of his performance, but would make it a D because he tried so hard. She told him that he had no command of the English language and absolutely no ability to communicate through speaking or writing.

All of us in the seminar laughed, since he had held us in the palm of his hand through his speaking ability. In addition to being a successful businessman, he is the author of several books and is a popular motivational speaker, having appeared on many local and national television programs. Ironically, Western Kentucky University observed "Stan Cottrell Week," with the governor and numerous other state officials present. Stan gave the keynote address—and his speech teacher was seated in the audience.

How has Stan climbed every mountain of opportunity despite formidable odds? I believe the answer may be found in a Chinese legend of fire and jade that I heard him discuss on another occasion. He said the Chinese explain the principle of balance by comparing it to a windwheel. The two blades are opposite, opposing forces. But when they are in balance, they turn with what seems like effortless power.

His fire has come from determination, enthusiasm, and a belief that God has given him special gifts to be used to help others and to glorify God. The jade has come through quiet self-renewal in faith, clear thinking, and an absolute assurance that he is "specialer."

36

Expect God's Surprises

It was at Duke Chapel on the campus of Duke University many years ago that I heard Albert Outler's speech, "Look For and Expect God's Surprises in Your Life." I was a young adult who had not developed the art of awareness. Often I found myself being moody, negative, and sometimes blasé. Dr. Outler's words revolutionized my thinking. They helped me look for the presence of God in the here and now, and in the ordinary experiences of life.

"When I awaken each morning," said the eminent Christian theologian, "I ask, 'God, what surprises do you have in store for me today?'" For background, he used the biblical story of Moses seeing the bush that burned and was not consumed. He said, "God instructed Moses to take off his shoes because he was standing on holy ground. He did that before God gave him the important call to head the children of Israel out of Egypt." Then Dr. Outler quoted Elizabeth Barrett Browning:

> Earth's crammed with heaven,
> And every common bush aflame with God;
> But only he who sees takes off his shoes.
> The rest sit round it and pluck blackberries . . . .

Seated in the Duke Chapel that day, I determined I would look for God's surprises, that I would look for the sacred amid the secular, that I would not just spend my life sitting around plucking blackberries. Yet I hadn't recently thought of that long-ago incident until some of God's surprises were so evident. I was part of a nine-member team that gathered in Birmingham, Alabama. Our assignment was to travel to four different sections of the state—Birmingham, Huntsville, Gadsden, and Alexander City—to present training seminars in churches.

On the flight from Atlanta to Birmingham, my seatmate was an attractive, vivacious woman in her early forties. She told me that she had been away for two weeks on business for the company for which she worked. When she learned that I was going to be helping churches to launch and sustain a ministry geared toward single adults, she said, "Let me tell you some of the woes of a blended family."

She regaled me with humorous and poignant stories about rearing children from two different households. It was certainly an enlightening glimpse into the real struggles of blended families, and made me realize why so many second marriages fail. While we waited for our luggage, I asked if she would keep an eye on my briefcase while I called for the shuttle to my hotel.

"Oh, I'm planning to take you to your hotel," she said authoritatively.

With surprise, I replied, "I can't let you go out of your way to take me there. After being away for two weeks, I'm sure you are eager to get home" (though after all she had told me, I wasn't so sure that was a true statement).

She insisted, and we loaded our luggage into her new sports car and took off. I said a brief prayer: "Thank you, Lord, for a nice surprise—a new insight, a new friend, and door-to-door delivery to my hotel."

On Sunday we were scheduled to complete the training in Alexander City at 7:00 P.M., drive back to Birmingham, and go our separate ways on Monday. Following an 8:30 worship service Sunday morning, we heard the news of the approaching ice and sleet. The storm was scheduled to arrive in Birmingham in the early evening. Our leaders decided to close the session in Alexander City at 5:00 P.M. to enable participants to drive home safely, and the instructors to make earlier flight connections.

Unfortunately, I could not get a flight back to Atlanta that evening. Then came another of God's neat surprises. Realizing my predicament, John, a college professor and a member of our team came up to me and said, "Nell, if you don't mind riding in my pickup truck, I'll take you to Atlanta, and maybe you can get a flight to Chattanooga."

Laughing, I replied, "John, I'd love that, so long as I don't have to ride in the back of the truck."

So, dressed professionally in a suit and heels, I climbed up in the passenger seat of a pickup truck. As we sped through the small towns and over the back roads of Alabama and Georgia, I thought to myself, *And I thought retirement was going to be boring.*

John is the same age as my son—a part of the baby boomer generation. He attended seminary in the early 1970s, and his interests are as diverse as his choices in transportation. In addition, he is an engaging conversationalist. Our subjects ranged from family to education, to campus and national politics, to our dreams for the Christian church in America.

The conversation was so stimulating that I didn't get apprehensive about making my flight in Atlanta. When he deposited my bag at Delta's baggage check-in, I had less than ten minutes to get to my gate. With my coat flying wildly and my high heels clicking as I ran, I made record time and arrived at the gate just as they were announcing the final call for the flight to Chattanooga.

Continuing my mad dash down the jetway, I found the one seat left, buckled my seat belt, and we began our taxi down the runway. Putting my head back and closing my eyes, I said silently, "Lord, that was almost too close for comfort, but I thank you for another of your surprises."

On Monday when I awakened in Chattanooga to ice and sleet and snow, I gave thanks again for being home, and for Albert Outler's suggestion that we should look for and expect God's surprises.

37

Fully Alive?

"COME ALIVE TO REAL LIFE." THOSE WERE THE FIRST WORDS OF A devotional I read on January 1, and I hope will be the guide by which I can evaluate my days.

Zorba the Greek, in the movie by the same name, said, "The only death is a day that is not fully lived." Moses, as he gave God's covenant to the children of Israel just before they moved into the promised land, said, "I have set before you life and death, blessing and curse: therefore choose life" (Deut. 30:19). Jesus' plan for living is summarized in his statement: "I am come that [you] might have life . . . and have it more abundantly" (John 10:10).

Why then do we face life only half alive—blind to the beauty around us, limited by our lack of vision and faith, and imprisoned by inertia, negative emotions, and fear of failure?

In the past, as I have experimented in my own life and observed others, I have discovered several things that contribute to aliveness. In the first place, taking care of our bodies is essential. We have just one chance at life, and this is it. Several years ago, the National Dairy Association used a catchy tune in advertising: "There's a new you coming every day." The inference was that cells in our body are being born all the time, and every seven years we get completely new bodies, with a few exceptions. I don't know about you, but I keep hoping that I get a better-looking body during the next seven years. I'd also like one that won't get fat when I eat too much, and won't get stiff when I don't exercise.

Yet, the truth is that if we want to be fully alive we have to maintain and care for our bodies. That means eating nutritionally, sleeping enough, avoiding excesses, and exercising regularly.

In the same way, we need to keep mentally fit. The late E. Stanley Jones said in one of his messages, "You don't grow old. You get old because you don't grow." To be fully alive, we need to read widely, study, observe, and adapt to changes. It has been said that most of us use only one-third of our mental capacities. I am certain that one of the reasons for that is that we so easily get bogged down in trivia.

Mental fitness also involves choosing our thoughts carefully. The Scripture reminds us that "as [a man] thinketh in his heart, so is he." Paul admonishes us to think on things that are pure, true, lovely, of good report. In other words, just as we feed our bodies with nourishing food, we need to feed our minds with positive, energizing thoughts of faith, hope, and love, rather than with negative, defeating thoughts of ill will. Thoughts are living things, and they do determine our destinies. Therefore we should choose life-giving thoughts. Persons who are alive also set goals for living. They don't just drift, being at the mercy of whatever external circumstances may occur. Instead, they determine the value system under which they will live (for me, this is the Christian faith). In accordance with their values, they set goals for daily and long-term living. Napoleon Hill's *The Science of Personal Achievement* (Simon & Schuster, 1993) records his study of five hundred Americans who were recognized as most successful in their fields. They were different in terms of background and philosophy, but they all believed in the importance of goal setting.

These successful people also agreed on the necessity of taking risks, and of failing. Many people limit their aliveness by their fear of failure. All of the successful people I know have failed many times, but they don't stop with their failures. They bounce back and move ahead. Dr. Hill said that many of the successful people he interviewed had their greatest failure just before their biggest success.

Fully alive people reach out to others in caring, affirmation, and compassion. How wonderful that God planned for us to be born in families. Obviously God didn't mean for us to be lonely, alienated human beings. We are far more alive to life when our inner worlds touch others in a significant way.

Finally, and most important, we come most fully alive when our lives are brought into alignment with the purposes of God. It is God who calls us to life and creativity. Only through him can we become "fully alive"!

38

Want a Happy "Forever"?

WHILE IN FLORIDA FOR A SPEAKING ENGAGEMENT, I SAW A BUMPER sticker that read: "Have a happy forever." That very evening, after I finished speaking, a couple came to the front of the church and asked for an appointment to talk. The next day when we kept the appointment, I looked carefully at the handsome couple as they spoke. He was a tall, soft-spoken, "Southern gentleman" type, with a shock of wavy gray hair. She, as he, was in her eighties, though she walked with the agility of a woman in her fifties. She was dressed in a rose-colored linen suit, and her slightly lined, smiling face was framed by softly coifed gray hair. It was she who spoke first.

"This may seem strange to you because we are people of faith, but we are not sure about life after death. My husband has cancer, and the doctors say that he will not live long, so we need some reassurance."

Before I could reply, the soft-spoken man spoke with sudden firmness. "I want to ask a simple question, and I don't want any theological gobbledygook—just a straightforward, unequivocal 'yes' or 'no.'"

"That's fair enough," I replied. "You ask a straight question, and I will give you a straight answer."

"If we are Christians, when we die, will we live again? Will we be reunited with each other?"

"The answer is 'yes.'"

"How sure are you?"

"Absolutely, positively, 100 percent sure."

"Why are you so sure?" the man asked with a sense of urgency.

I proceeded to tell him the reasons for my certainty, that the Bible clearly teaches life after death for those who love the Lord and have experienced his grace. I quoted such passages as John 14:19 ("Because I live, [you] shall live also") and John 11:25-16 ("I am the resurrection, and the life: he that believeth in me, though he were dead, yet shall he live: And whosoever liveth and believeth in me shall never die"). I reminded him of how Jesus appeared to many, and that his own resurrection had impeccable proof.

Then I remembered a parable and an incident told by Cecil B. DeMille, one of the most famous motion picture directors in Hollywood. He was also a very sensitive and spiritual man. The parable was about a baby in a prenatal state, tucked up under a mother's loving heart. "Suppose," I said, "that someone might come to this unborn baby and say, 'You cannot stay here very long. In a few months you will be born, or you will die out of this present state.' The baby might stubbornly remonstrate, 'I don't want to leave here. I am comfortable, I'm well cared for, I am warm, loved, and happy. I don't want to leave this place.'

"But in the normal course of events he is born. He does die out of his mother's womb. What does he find? He feels beneath him strong, loving arms. He looks up into a beautiful face, tender with love, and the face of his mother. He is welcomed, cuddled, cared for. He might say, 'How foolish I was. This is a wonderful place to which I have come.'

"Then the child grows into manhood, marries, rears his own children, enjoys achievements of middle age, and becomes an old man. One day a doctor may say to him, 'You cannot stay here. You are going to die, or be born out of this place into another.' And he might remonstrate, 'But I don't want to die. It is warm and pleasant here, and I have my loved ones.'

"But there comes a time when he does die. What happens then? Is God going to change his nature? Can we not assume that the man will once again feel loving arms beneath him, and once again look up into a strong, beautiful face, more lovely than the first face he saw so long ago? Won't he soon be exclaiming, 'This new life is wonderful. I want to remain here forever.'"

"That makes sense to me," replied the man, "but what is the incident you mentioned?"

It was this story: Cecil B. DeMille, having discovered that his canoe had drifted into shallow water while he was working on a script, saw on the lake bottom a large number of water beetles. One of them crawled out of the water, sank his talons into the hull of the boat, and died.

Three hours later, the film director observed an amazing miracle. The shell of the water beetle cracked open; a moist head emerged, followed by wings; and finally, the winged creature left the dead body and flew into the air, going farther in one half second than the water beetle could have crawled all day. The dragonfly flew above the surface of the water, but the water beetles below could not see it.

"Do you think the Almighty God would do this for a water beetle and wouldn't do this for human beings—the highest of his creations?" I asked.

Smiling, the couple nodded their heads in understanding. "It's what we have believed in our minds, and now we believe in our hearts," said the man. "Yes," replied the woman, "Now we are ready to celebrate Easter."

39

Take an Inch at a Time

DISORDER, CONFUSION, CHAOS! I DISLIKE ALL THREE, BUT FELT CATA-pulted into them recently as my husband and I cleaned out our library. Stacks of articles that each of us had marked and saved for years; stacks of *National Geographic* and other magazines; books that were loved but no longer current, and needed to be given away or recycled so that our library could have some order again.

Suddenly I had a flashback of the day after we moved to Kingsport, Tennessee, in 1981. I was looking into a room piled high with boxes, and was feeling overwhelmed. The things that helped me in 1981 helped me recently in our library. It occurred to me that what I needed to do in this situation is what we need to do in our personal lives when we have painted ourselves into a corner, or have come to an unexpected detour, or are feeling overwhelmed by circumstances.

First, I remembered not to panic. Panic destroys quiet. It uses all our psychic energy for negative emotions—fear, anger, distress, frustration. It prevents moving forward to face whatever we must. Instead, we bog down into inertia, or make uncertain, ineffective, even contradictory, moves. We become like the man who mounted a horse and rode off in all directions.

So, when I was tempted, I chose not to panic. I took some deep breaths, became quiet at the center of my being, and thanked God for every good thing I could think of, including God's providential care in the past. In fact, I used the quick-help prayer of Louise Mohr, that dynamic Christian leader who spoke often at Faith-at-Work Conferences. The prayer consists of nine words: "Lord, I can't. You can. Please do. Thanks! Amen."

Then as peace began to come over me, I used the divine gift of imagination. I visualized the room as it was going to look when everything was in place. Even when the task seemed endless, I kept that picture before me. It is amazing how easy it is to organize and move toward something if you can see where you are going.

Then, as I worked, I remembered the words of a neighbor to someone who was procrastinating about cleaning out a cluttered garage. The advice: "Why don't you clean out one corner at a time?" In other words, instead of being overwhelmed by the total task, divide it into manageable portions and complete them one at a time.

This is true with life. A young woman with three small children told me once, when I asked how she accounted for her evident joy in marriage, "My husband and I have a special night out once every two weeks, and you can stand anything for two weeks! When the children are sick or fretful, or when the dishes are piled high in the sink, I keep thinking, 'Only two more weeks and I can get out.'" If at any point she had thought of all the dishes she would have to wash, or diapers she would have to change during the lifetime of marriage, she would have felt like throwing in the towel.

Alcoholics Anonymous teaches its members the value of living in even shorter time segments. They encourage members to stay sober one day at a time. Short-term goals make the long-term goals reachable. The quotation, "Life by the yard is hard, but life by the inch is a cinch," is applicable to all of life.

Another thing that made my week of clutter bearable in 1981 was love made visible through the tangible actions of friends—both old and new. Two friends came and helped with the actual unpacking; new friends stopped by with food and cheery greetings; flowers and notes came, saying, "We are thinking of you." It was from a tow-headed ten-year-old that we received the biggest lift. He wheeled into our driveway on his ten-speed, came to the door, and jauntily introduced himself by saying, "Hi. I'm Bo. I'm your next-door neighbor, and I'm glad you moved to Kingsport. Garbage day is Tuesday, and you need to take the bags to the street for pickup."

That was all. With a cheery "See ya," he was on his bike and gone. Yet my heart felt lighter when he left.

So when you are overwhelmed with disorder, don't panic. God can bring order out of disorder—if you become quiet and trust God's leadership; if you take one step at a time; and if you learn to see God's love through the kindness of friends.

40

The Power of Anticipation

MOST OF US LEARN EARLY IN LIFE THAT THE ANTICIPATION OF AN event—a trip, a party, a graduation, a wedding—is almost as much fun as the event itself. The anticipation overshadows and makes less important the dull and boring, but necessary, tasks of everyday living.

Soon after my husband and I were married, he suggested that we always plan something to which we could look forward every two weeks. Often it was something as simple as having friends over for dessert, or going to a movie. This was especially important when the children were small.

We tried to incorporate the same thing into our family life—a picnic, swimming, a trip to the skating rink, or other age-related interests. We learned that children finish necessary chores much more quickly if they are anticipating a fun experience. After our retirement, we continued this practice in a short Thanksgiving holiday trip with our son, daughter-in-law, and grandchildren.

So, as we made plans for the birthday dinner for our son and daughter-in-law (they have July birthdays only fifteen days apart), I decided we would have a "let's go to London" party in anticipation of this year's trip. Even planning the party was fun. Thanks to the travel agency, we had posters on the front door and throughout the house. A friend brought stacks of beautiful booklets that described in words and pictures the places we would be visiting, from Westminster Abbey and the Tower of London to Buckingham Palace, Harrods, and the theater district. There were booklets of British history and the story of British royalty. I learned more about the British Empire from our friend's booklets than from our former visits to England, including a summer's ministerial exchange in 1986. She also brought us some shortbread fingers (most of which disappeared before the dinner was held).

An English dinner began to take shape through the help of a

Harrod's cookbook and the English Rose Tearoom. The flowers on the serving table were in an English teapot with small Union Jack flags on each side. The dinner included roast beef, English vegetables, and a salad. The birthday cake was a huge English trifle. Instead of the usual layers of cake—vanilla pudding, fruit, and whipped cream—we used chocolate cake, chocolate pudding, and Heath Bars crumpled up on each layer of cream. It was sinfully good!

After we participated in the usual after-dinner ritual of each telling the honorees what we most appreciate about them, and before they sat in the birthday chair to receive their cards and presents, everyone played an English matchup game. It was a fun evening. Even more, I, who had inwardly resisted our taking a trip to London in November (too cold), ended the evening counting the days until we leave on Thanksgiving Day.

It occurred to me that if anticipation creates enthusiasm and excitement, why don't we use it more in our families, our jobs, our schools, and churches? This requires a positive expectancy and the belief that we can do something to make it happen.

Recently Dr. John Claypool IV, speaking at our church, reminded us of an event in the life of Arthur Gordon, a well-known Christian author. Gordon, a high achiever throughout his life, experienced two crushing defeats in his midthirties that thrust him into deep depression. His parents persuaded him to see a psychotherapist who was an old family friend.

After listening to his patient reiterate his problems and thus internalize them, the therapist said that he would work with Gordon if he would change two phrases—if instead of saying "if only" (living regretfully in the past) he would say "next time" (allowing him to anticipate the future). That simple change was the catalyst for turning the brilliant young man's life around.

When I am tempted to bog down in regret, I think of God saying through Moses to the children of Israel as they stood before the Red Sea—before the waters parted—and with Pharaoh's army hot in pursuit: "Speak unto the children of Israel, that they go forward" (Exod. 14:15). I believe God says the same thing to us today, and a part of that process is our anticipation.

41

Helped Any "Ciphers" Lately?

IT WAS NOT HARD TO GUESS THAT HE WAS A LONER. HIS THIN, SENSI-tive face and the faraway look in his eyes were the first clues. If you observed him at school—in the classroom, on the playground, or even on the school bus—it was obvious that he always sat alone and talked with no one.

But that was the problem: no one did observe Terry. Though he was thirteen years of age and had ridden the same school bus since he was in the third grade, no one recognized his body after he had asked to get off the bus and fell dead in the snow. As they waited for the ambulance to arrive, the bus driver found Terry's name in one of his books. But later, at the school, the principal was not able to put a name with a face. No one in the office remembered the boy. It was almost as if he were a zero—as if he had been erased from the memory of his peers and teachers. In fact, the teacher who was asked to check his school records, made that statement. He said, "Through indifference and neglect, the personality of this shy, sensitive child was erased a little at a time by fellow students, teachers, and particularly a sullen stepfather, who refused to adopt the boy."

Actually, Mark, the math teacher who checked the records, had been asked to do so because Terry had written that Mark was his favorite teacher.

"His favorite teacher?" Mark exclaimed in surprise when the principal revealed this to him. "I hardly knew the boy, though I do remember helping him a couple of times with math problems. If I was his favorite teacher, he must have had a pitiful school experience."

When the records were placed before Mark, he noted that Terry's first-grade teacher had written: "He is a shy child, but eager to learn." The second teacher had echoed those words and added: "He likes to help others." It was the third-grade teacher who wrote:

"Terry looks out the window and daydreams too much. He is a slow learner." Almost incidentally she had added: "He seems pained by his parents' divorce." From that point on, teachers each year had written words like *withdrawn*, *lacks social skills*, *dull*, *indifferent*.

When Mark drove to the small house where the boy had lived, he found a frail, submissive woman and her sullen, abusive, beer-guzzling husband. The woman began to cry quietly when she learned of Terry's death. "He was a good boy," she said.

"He was not a good boy," bellowed the stepfather from his chair in front of the TV. "Terry was lazy and disobedient." Then he told of how Terry had been "stupid enough to bring home willow branches from a walk just the day before, instead of shoveling the snowy walks as he had been commanded to do."

"I knocked those stupid branches out of his hand and told him how dumb and no good he was, but it didn't do any good."

For Mark, the climate of the home was even more evident when the unassertive woman put on her coat and went toward the door. "Hey, where are you going?" the man yelled.

"I'm going to see my son," she replied in a firm, almost defiant tone.

"What about my breakfast?" he asked as the door closed quietly behind his wife. The man's beady eyes narrowed as he reached for the beer can and boasted, "She'll regret this."

The coroner's report was inconclusive. The doctors could find no reason for the sudden death of this unknown thirteen-year-old. Mark, however, knew that the boy had died of a broken heart. He could no longer face the loneliness, the pain, the torture of having his personality erased—of being a zero.

Mark remembered the babies who had died in hospitals from lack of love and human touch, though they had warm beds and plenty of milk. He thought, *Even teenagers can die from being ignored and from verbal abuse.* He made a commitment to himself as he stood by Terry's grave. *I may not be able to teach math to every student who comes into my classroom, but not one of them will ever leave feeling that he or she is a zero.*

The above is the scenario for a video entitled *Cipher in the Snow*.

It is presumably based upon a true story. Whether it is true or not, the video was so moving that it caused me to reevaluate my own interpersonal relationships.

In a fast-paced world where we are apt to be preoccupied with our own interests or simply doing what comes next, how many times do we "pass by on the other side" when we see a lonely, hurting person? How many times are children neglected when parents forget the children need to have their spirits fed as well as their bodies? Little people don't open the doors of their hearts too often to grown-ups. If we miss the moment or fail to sense their questions or pain, we slowly erase a part of their potential.

It is staggering to recognize that suicide is the second most common reason for teenage deaths. No longer can we speak of youth as being the carefree time of life. Far too many are encased in such despair that life seems to hold nothing.

When you add to this the emotional homicides that are occurring in marriages, families, schools, and places of employment, you realize that "Cipher in the Snow" is not farfetched in its message. All of us need to sharpen our skills of sensitivity, and hear again the Word of God: "Bear ye one another's burdens, and so fulfil the law of Christ" (Gal. 6:2).

42

At the Doctor's Office

THE PLAY ENTITLED *A FUNNY THING HAPPENED ON THE WAY TO THE Forum* popped into my mind as a funny thing happened to me at the doctor's office. The only similarity between the two was that in each case something unexpected happened. As for the play, which is written by Burt Shevelove and Larry Gelbart, people went expecting outstanding music and were surprised by the unexpected humor and hilarity. I was surprised by the unexpected gift of appreciation.

Much of life involves waiting, whether at a doctor's office, dentist's office, or even the ordering lane at a fast-food restaurant. As a result, I habitually take a briefcase full of letters or speeches to be written, as well as a cellular phone and a list of people I need to call. That morning was no exception. Although my appointment was at 8:00, there was already a room full of patients when I arrived. So I pulled out my trusty, though slightly beaten-up, briefcase. Engrossed in my work, I was totally oblivious to my surroundings. As I hesitated for a moment in my writing, I heard a female voice say, "When you take time for a deep breath, I'd like to tell you something."

Glancing over to my left, I looked into the warm and friendly face of a woman I had never seen before. She introduced herself as Shirley from Georgia. She thanked me for my Sunday articles and told me that she had a scrapbook full of them. She also told me that her husband died after a ten-year struggle with cancer. The disease was in various parts of his body, but it was brain cancer that finally took his life.

Then she became specific about the articles that meant the most to her during that time. She mentioned the ones I had written about attitudes, encouragement, faith, and particularly the ones in which I shared my own struggle with this devious disease called cancer. The funny thing that happened was that I had come into the doctor's office feeling fatigued and not too well. By the time I was called back to the examining room, I was already feeling better. The medicine had been a dose of sincere and unexpected appreciation.

Suddenly it occurred to me that the things I had always believed about appreciation were absolutely true. Sincere appreciation lifts the spirit, motivates, provides hope, and allows the recipient to renew his or her belief in themselves. Then I thought of the persons who have influenced my life for good. They were people who obviously saw my faults, but believed in me anyway and helped me to believe in myself. This didn't mean that they didn't correct me or offer constructive suggestions. But they did these things without anger and in an ambiance of appreciation. Among the many people who have done this for me are my paternal grandmother, who seemed to enjoy my company; my father, who told me that God had put a treasure in me; a special friend who expressed appreciation for every small gift of kindness I offered; a youth counselor who constantly met my uncertainties with the words "You can do it, Nell, you can do it! "; my husband, who is a cheerleader for every endeavor I undertake; my son and daughter-in-law, whose cards and letters leave me feeling appreciated; my grandchildren, whose very presence motivates me to be more than I am.

The late William James, Harvard sociologist and psychologist, wrote: "Imagine that everyone you meet is wearing a sign reading, 'I want to be appreciated.'" The great apostle Paul wrote to the Ephesians (4:32), "Be ye kind one to another." He surely must have known that kindness is a component of expressed appreciation. The funny thing is that we each have the power to lift the spirits of others. We have the power, through sincere appreciation, to motivate and enable others to believe in themselves. Let's use the power.

43

Thank God for Chemotherapy

FROM THE DAY I LEARNED I HAD A MALIGNANCY, I RESISTED THE thought of taking chemotherapy. The thought of such powerful drugs invading my body was unthinkable to me.

Also, the possible side effects were frightening—nausea, loss of hair, depleted energy, dryness and soreness of the mouth, swelling of the extremities, lowered resistance to infection, and in some cases, anemia and kidney problems. Just the possibility of these side effects is enough to make you opt for letting the cancer grow.

During my first few treatments, I considered chemotherapy my enemy and steeled myself to grin and bear it. Each month when I entered the hospital (such heavy doses were prescribed that they required an overnight stay), I inwardly went into battle against them. I disliked their power and resented having to go through such traumatic experiences. By the time I left the hospital, my neck and shoulders were in knots, and my stomach felt like a dump heap of heavy metal.

It was in my prayer time one day that I suddenly saw this treatment as my ally, my friend. It was as if God were saying to me, "I am sending you help in excellent doctors and nurses and chemotherapy. Cooperate with them, if you want to be well again." From that point on, my entire attitude changed 180 degrees. It didn't mean that I looked forward eagerly to the treatments; far from it! But I learned to cooperate with rather than fight against them.

During that time, for three weeks out of each month, I resumed my usual schedule—speaking, writing, teaching Sunday school, traveling, enjoying family and friends, even entertaining. During those weeks I didn't even think about chemotherapy. I tried to live with energy, joy, and enthusiasm. If I had a passing thought about the next treatment, I saw it as an inconvenience, but one that would help me back to health and vitality. I replaced those thoughts with constructive ones about what I was doing that particular day.

When the fourth week arrived, I went to the doctor's office for the weekly blood test, followed that day by a physical examination. From there I entered the hospital. In the beginning I resisted that— later I could say laughingly to the nurses in the doctor's office, "Well, I am checking into the luxury hotel again." Even that change of emphasis helped my thinking.

Even before going to the doctor's office the morning of the treatment, I would take time to thank God for chemotherapy, and I prayed that I would cooperate willingly and gratefully in all the procedures that would follow. When the IV's started, I visualized those powerful drugs attacking each of the tiny cancer cells and killing them on contact. Though intravenous needles have always been a bugaboo to me (and especially since it gets progressively harder to find a vein that hasn't collapsed), I always believed that there was a good one available, and there was. I envisioned the enormous amount of fluid that goes through my system as a cleansing agent, keeping the drugs from doing damage to the vital organs which would cause renal failure.

Actually, I realize that control of my thoughts and emotions was easier for me because I did not suffer many of the frightening side effects. For example, I did not lose my hair, though it did become noticeably thinner. I did not have to wear a wig—which alone is a tremendous boost for a woman. Nausea, fatigue, weakness, and an occasional swelling of my legs were my side effects. Though they were not easy, they certainly were bearable one week out of four.

In addition to a change in my attitude, and a commitment on my part to cooperate with the treatments, some other things have helped on what to me is a journey through uncharted waters. For one thing, my oncologist and his staff, as well as the nurses and medical personnel on the hospital's third floor, have continued their same quality of professional competence and personal compassion that was evidenced both during and after my surgery. Also, my husband has been my special nurse at the hospital, spending each night there with me except one, when he had to be out of town. My friend Sally volunteered to be there in his place and eased my fears in her usual calm and comforting manner. My husband, Ralph, was not only there, but was at home with me when I needed cold cloths and soothing words during bouts with nausea.

My network of support always includes our son and his wife, who despite busy schedules came to visit each time I was in the hospital. The ministers from our church came and offered beautiful prayers. Other friends, learning that I was to have another treatment, sent notes, cards, and food. The love and support of these persons was crucial in providing encouragement during seemingly interminable months.

Most of all, God's presence has never been more real to me. It has given me strength to keep on "hanging in there," it has given me comfort when I grow weary, it has given me guidance—such as the idea of cooperating with instead of fighting the chemotherapy. Always I am reminded of God's promise in Psalm 89:33: "Nevertheless (whatever happens) My lovingkindness I will not utterly take from [you], nor allow My faithfulness to fail" (NKJV).

Today I have "lived" with my cancer and "overcome" my cancer for the last seven years. I am never unmindful that God's lovingkindness and faithfulness continue to be my source of strength and support.